Endorsements

"Life Unhindered! reveals the truth about what it means to live in freedom. Jennifer Kennedy Dean has given us a profound guide that offers a biblical, practical, life-altering method for tapping into the limitless resources available to every Christian who longs to experience transformation. I highly recommend this book!"—Carol Kent, speaker and author of *When I Lay My Isaac Down*

"Life Unhindered! explores a number of biblical and historical accounts of individuals who threw aside all of the hindrances in life that were barriers to following God's plan. Through a close look at Scripture, Jennifer reminds us that the power to successfully navigate life's circumstances comes from one source only—the God who loves us and promises His presence in every situation. Living a *Life Unhindered!* opens up all the possibilities for finding and fulfilling the promises of God each day as we engage our world in discovering the truth of how God wants us to live."—Wanda Lee, executive director, WMU

"Jennifer Kennedy Dean redefines the conventional definition of freedom in *Life Unhindered!* She readily convinces her readers that true freedom doesn't come from being who we want to be, but in becoming who God created us to be. Our soul's deepest desire for freedom is satisfied in the ability to live with abandonment to God's call in our lives."—Jill Rigby Garner, author of *Raising Unselfish Children in a Self-Absorbed World*

"Life Unhindered! moves the reader into appreciating and living out the freedom Jesus died to give us. Jennifer hands us the keys to our freedom and our future—inspiring us all along the way. I know Jennifer and she walks out her freedom in a way that everyone is a better person for knowing her or reading her words."—Pam Farrel, author of more than 30 books, including *Men Are Like Waffles, Women Are Like Spaghetti; Woman of Confidence;* and *Woman of Influence*

Life Unhindered!

Five Keys to
Walking in Freedom

JENNIFER KENNEDY DEAN

NEW HOPE
PUBLISHERS
BIRMINGHAM, ALABAMA

New Hope® Publishers
P. O. Box 12065
Birmingham, AL 35202-2065
www.newhopepublishers.com
New Hope Publishers is a division of WMU®

Library of Congress Cataloging-in-Publication Data

Dean, Jennifer Kennedy.
  Life unhindered! : five keys to walking in freedom / Jennifer Kennedy Dean.
    p. cm.
  ISBN-13: 978-1-59669-286-2 (sc)
  ISBN-10: 1-59669-286-3 (sc)
  1. Christian life. 2. Liberty--Religious aspects--Christianity. 3. Christian life--Biblical teaching. 4. Liberty--Biblical teaching. I. Title.
  BV4509.5.D425 2010
  248.4--dc22
                        2009053300

Cover design: J. R. Caines, www.cainesdesign.com
Interior design: Sherry Hunt

ISBN-10: 1-59669-286-3
ISBN-13: 978-1-59669-286-2
N104143 • 0410 • 6M1

Dedication

To those whose lives have borne witness to me of the faithfulness of God. In particular,

My parents, the late Don Kennedy and Audrey Kennedy, who lived out integrity and unconditional love and passion for Jesus and His church.

My late brother, Roger Quin Kennedy, who taught me what courage and selflessness look like when the flame of life's crucible is turned up high.

My late husband, Wayne Dean, whose kindness and gentleness never faltered, and who leaves behind much fruit—fruit that will last into the final generation.

Contents

Acknowledgments

I want to thank Joshua Hearne for allowing me use of his research into the lives of historical Christian figures. His passion for researching the lives of those whose examples shape the church today can be seen in his blog, http://www.ttstm.com/. You will enjoy and benefit from making his blog a resource for your spiritual life.

Always, always, I must thank the entire staff at New Hope. They are not just publishers, but partners in ministry. They bring to each book a passion for its message.

The Freedom March

Every human desires freedom. No race of people has ever been content to be enslaved or even to have their freedom limited. Lack of freedom always gives rise to a liberation movement.

My sons always loved the movie *Braveheart* about Scottish freedom fighter William Wallace who led in the First War of Scottish Independence. In the movie, Mel Gibson played the title role. Their favorite scene consisted of the fierce Scottish warriors in garish war paint, armed with a plethora of weapons, with William Wallace in the lead position. He shouts, "They may take our lives, but they'll never take our freedom!" As he shouts the word *freedom* at the top of his lungs, the warriors surge forward to fight against incalculable odds. All for freedom. The final scene has Wallace on the scaffold about to be decapitated. As the ax falls, he shouts, "Freedom!"

Freedom! Our hearts all shout it. We are never completely at home in conditions that limit or rob us of our freedom. Something in us rebels and finds little ways, at least, to exercise some freedom. Freedom is encoded in the fiber of our personalities. It is the state to which we naturally aspire. Where it is lacking, we long for it, seek it, dream of it, work for it. History is filled with freedom movements, wars fought for freedom, freedom won, and freedom lost. The ingrained, built-in desire to be free is shared by human beings of all cultures, all ages, all nations.

Slavery or imprisonment comes in all shapes and sizes. A person physically shackled and imprisoned can be inwardly free. A person with no restrictions imposed on his liberty can be enslaved within. True freedom is provided by Christ, and apart from Him no one can be truly free. "It is for freedom that Christ has set us free" (Galatians 5:1). "If the Son sets you free, you will be free indeed" (John 8:36).

Freedom is Christ's goal for your life, so your spiritual enemy and his realm have targeted your freedom and work against it with energy and craftiness. Ingeniously, the enemy's forces strategize to limit or even steal your freedom. Whatever God wants you to experience, your enemy wants you to miss out on. Whatever God wants you to believe, your enemy wants you to doubt. Whatever God wants you to know, your enemy wants you to be ignorant about. God wants you free. Your enemy wants you bound.

What does real freedom look like? People who are free in Christ will be free to reach out to the world around them with God's love. Certain of their own position and provision, free people can live poured-out lives. Truly free people will

- be vehicles through which God's Spirit will be unleashed in the world;
- be leaders of influence and uncompromised integrity;
- be courageous in their calling and engaged in their culture;
- be passionate about God as they step out and take risks together with other believers.

EXPERIENCING FREEDOM

The purifying process that begins at the moment of salvation and continues into eternity is God's way of making you fully free. Freedom is not just a concept, but instead should be your daily experience. Jesus has provided full-spectrum salvation. Nothing about your humanity is left out of the salvation journey. At every level of your life and in every layer of your being—mind, will, emotions, relationships, habits, ministry—Jesus wants you to be free.

Jesus wants you free so that you can freely serve others—pouring into the lives of others what He has poured into yours. You can't pour water from a dry vessel. Jesus wants to clean you out and fill you up so that you can be His vessel in a desperate and hurting world.

Look at Jesus's words in John 13:12–17.

When he had finished washing their feet, he put on his clothes and returned to his place. "Do you understand what I have done for you?" he asked them. "You call me 'Teacher' and 'Lord,' and rightly so, for that is what I am. Now that I, your Lord and Teacher, have washed your feet, you also should wash one another's feet. I have set you an example that you should do as I have done for you. I tell you the truth, no servant is greater than his master, nor is a messenger greater than the one who sent him. Now that you know these things, you will be blessed if you do them."

Pay close attention to how Jesus prefaces His call to imitate His servant actions. "Now that I, your Lord and Teacher, have washed your feet." Unless Jesus has first touched our lives, we have nothing to offer others. What did He tell us to do? "You should do as I have done for you."

The purpose of foot washing was to cleanse away the dirt that clung to people's feet as they walked through the dusty streets. The foot washing to which Jesus referred—clearly meaning His act to be a metaphor—is the ongoing effect of our relationship with Him. He has cleansed us inside, but He is still washing away the grime that clings to us. "A person who has had a bath needs only to wash his feet; his whole body is clean. And you are clean" (John 13:10). He today works in our lives continually to cleanse and renew and restore and refresh so that we are free to be servants.

Look how the Scripture describes Jesus at that moment. "Jesus knew that the Father had put all things under his power, and that he had come from God and was returning to God; so he got up from the meal, took off his outer clothing, and wrapped a towel around his waist" (John 13:3–4). Because He knew the full power of God in His life, it freed Him to be a servant. Jesus wants us to be unhindered so that we, too, can be free to serve.

If Jesus died to make you free, and if your enemy works determinedly against your freedom, then surely God has laid out clearly His plan for winning that battle. God is not caught short. Is your enemy clever? He is. Is God immeasurably more clever? Oh yes. Is your enemy masterful at deception? He is. Is God immeasurably more masterful at unmasking deception with truth? Oh yes.

We are going to look at the keys that God has given us that open the door to the full freedom for which Christ died. We are going to examine these keys in detail and learn how to pick them up and use them to open the door to freedom and lock it behind us, denying the freedom-stealer any more access.

Here is our springboard:

> *Therefore, since we are surrounded by such a great cloud of witnesses, let us throw off everything that hinders and the sin that so easily entangles, and let us run with perseverance the race marked out for us. Let us fix our eyes on Jesus, the author and perfecter of our faith, who for the joy set before him endured the cross, scorning its shame, and sat down at the right hand of the throne of God.*
> —Hebrews 12:1–2

Let's break it down briefly to see how much these few Spirit-breathed words reveal about the freedom march to which we are called.

Key Number 1: His Platform

"Therefore" points us back to what has been said before. It serves as the explanation for what is about to be communicated. "Therefore, since we are surrounded by such a great cloud of witnesses." God has demonstrated His power through His work in the lives of His people. Our lives give Him a platform from which He can put His love and His power on display. He shows who He is by what He does. Look around. Observe the lives of those you know, and the lives of contemporary and historical figures, alongside the illustrations pointed to in Scripture. Be encouraged.

Throughout the book, I will reference the stories of contemporary and historical people, some famous and some not, who have lived or are living unhindered for Christ. I pray these stories of men and women will lead you to step out in faith too. (Note: I have changed some names to protect their privacy.)

Key Number 2: His Provision
"Let us throw off everything that hinders and the sin that so easily entangles." God never commands something of us that He has not provided for us. He provides the way out of every hindering habit, attitude, and belief.

Key Number 3: His Power
"Let us run with perseverance the race marked out for us." God empowers us to run the race that He has marked out for us. That race leads us in the path Jesus has run as our forerunner—right into the lives and needs of a hurting world.

Key Number 4: His Presence
"Let us fix our eyes on Jesus, the author and perfecter of our faith." His presence is our reference point. His indwelling life is continually available to us, and changes the focus of our whole lives.

Key Number 5: His Promise
"Who for the joy set before him endured the cross, scorning its shame, and sat down at the right hand of the throne of God." Our journey has a goal. The promise extends into eternity, but is not limited to the hereafter. He has a promise that is revealed in our lives day by day, moment by moment.

These are the themes that we will address in detail. As you read this book, incorporate its message. Stop and soak. Let the Holy Spirit speak His words into your situation and circumstances. Don't just absorb information. Lay your life out and let the Living Word examine it, reveal it, find its secrets, excavate it, pull back its layers, and mine its depths. Let the Word penetrate to the core of your life.

I pray that my inadequate words will be made more than adequate by the Living Word Himself. I pray that the words on the pages of this book will be words from the heart of the Father. I pray that the Holy Spirit will speak beyond the frailty of language and will convey His truth in power.

SUGGESTIONS FOR USING THIS BOOK IN A GROUP SETTING

This book provides you with two options for using the material as a small-group study, in addition to your individual use. Consider these as suggestions and ideas. Feel free to present and process the content in ways that fit your setting and the personality of your group. Use ideas from both options if you want.

Option 1: At the end of each chapter you will find small-group discussion and reflection questions. These should prompt sharing and ideas for application in your small group. At the end of each chapter, you will be challenged to reflect on the material in light of the four characteristics of truly free people found in this introduction (p. 12). Look for ways that some or all of these characteristics are referenced in each chapter.

Option 2: An alternative leader's guide can be found on pages 199–206. If your group responds to a more creative, innovative approach to absorbing the material, you will find ideas for a lively presentation, either as a weekly study or a weekend retreat.

Therefore, since we are surrounded by such a great cloud of witnesses...

Key 1
His Platform

CHAPTER 1

A Cloud of Witnesses

Our focal passage, Hebrews 12:1–2, opens with this phrase: "Therefore, since we are surrounded by so great a cloud of witnesses, let us throw aside every hindrance." These words follow on the heels of a passage in which the writer has listed men and women whose lives are examples of faith in action. It seems to me that the writer is saying that we should observe these examples of people who have thrown aside every hindrance and the sin which so easily besets, and do likewise. I would paraphrase it this way: "Since we have all these examples to follow, let's do the same things they did. Like them, let *us* throw aside every hindrance—the sin which so easily trips us up. And, like them, let *us* run the race set out for us." Earlier in the letter, the writer had said that we should imitate those who, by faith and patience, had inherited the promises (Hebrews 6:12). He is building on this theme.

He is pointing us to examples of lives that became His platform—the stage upon which He displayed His power and faithfulness. These examples were not chosen at random, but rather were deliberately inspired by the Spirit of God to illustrate faith in action. Not only are the examples mentioned by name, specific events in their lives are referenced. Exact. Concrete. In each example, the writer zooms in on a scene, isolating one detail of a larger canvas. This is carefully written so that any unnecessary scenes are left on the cutting room floor.

Every phrase matters. These exact scenes in these very lives tell the tale.

The single point is how faith works. In examining this passage in *Fueled by Faith*, I wrote: "It makes sense to me that if you observe how something functions, you then discover its definition. So, by observing faith in operation, I reach the conclusion that faith's central definition—its root definition—is 'obedience to the present-tense voice of the Lord.'...The Old Testament faithful are put on display as real-life lessons in how the faith principle operates. When God spoke, they acted in response to His voice, and God's power and provision flowed into the circumstances of earth and became visible."

The writer of Hebrews is addressing an audience familiar with each story. He knows he can allude to an event and his reader will know the details. He knows his audience will be able to connect all the dots. He can mention an event and his reader will be fully familiar with the context. It means he can speak to them in a sort of shorthand. With a few words, he can communicate volumes.

With this in mind, let's look at some of these incidents in the lives of our forerunners in faith, which the Holy Spirit isolated and spotlighted for our instruction. Let's be alert for what He is communicating to us about living life unhindered.

THE OPENING ACT

The first three illustrations in Hebrews 11 cover the time from the Creation through the Flood. These lives precede the nation of Israel and the giving of the Law. These men lived in the beginning of God's unfolding revelation. They responded to what they knew of God, and were held accountable and judged faithful based on the revelation they had received. As they embraced all of God they had glimpsed, God revealed even more. These men lived in the midst of a race and culture for whom God seemed distant and unknowable, yet these men knew Him. They experienced Him in real time and heard Him speak in present tense. Knowing Him meant understanding what God desired and doing what He commanded. That is the evidence of knowing God. Hearing and doing.

The Bible is the account of God's progressive revelation of Himself to mankind. He was fully revealed in Jesus, God made flesh. Jesus put God on full display. Nothing missing or hidden. "No one has ever seen God, but God the One and Only, who is at the Father's side, has made him known" (John 1:18). Paul puts it this way: "For in Christ all the fullness of the Deity lives in bodily form" (Colossians 2:9).

Even now, with Jesus in full view, God reveals Himself to us progressively as our minds and understanding can accommodate each new unfolding. The difference is that we are not starting from scratch. We have the Word of God in our hands and the fullness of the Spirit inside us, unveiling more and more of Jesus to our understanding each moment. The more we embrace and respond to what we have received, the more the Spirit reveals. The pattern holds.

Right now, have you fully embraced what God has revealed to you about Himself? Is there any obedience that God has called you to that you are resisting? Do you long to know God in His fullness? Are you willing to respond to Him now, driven by the hunger to know Him more?

Observe this trio of men and learn from their example. Why were these men and these incidents highlighted? How can you imitate their faith? What will the Living Word reveal to you about your heart, your life, your situation? "If anyone has ears to hear, let him hear" (Mark 4:23).

ABEL

"By faith Abel offered God a better sacrifice than Cain did. By faith he was commended as a righteous man, when God spoke well of his offerings. And by faith he still speaks, even though he is dead" (Hebrews 11:4).

Read the account to which this refers in Genesis 4:1–10. Even though you may know the story well, stop and read it with spiritual ears attentive to the Spirit.

I want to imagine for a moment. Don't you think it is safe to assume that both Cain and Abel had been told many times the story of the first time an animal was slain as a consequence of their sins? Their parents likely had told them about the days before the Fall, the idyllic days when Adam and Eve walked with God in the Garden and knew only life. In those days death was an unknown concept. Surely, in the telling, the parents expressed their horror at learning that their sin required a covering of blood, and a blood covering required that a beloved animal be killed as a substitute.

The first covering of blood was literal and personal. I think it's possible that the slain animal's skins, still wet with blood, were wrapped around the sinners, bloody side in direct contact with their bodies. Skin to skin. Literally covered by the blood. Blood still warm and wet with the life that had been offered. And a new reality was introduced: death. This scene would stay sharply focused in Adam and Eve's memory, not because it was gruesome, but because its effect was stunningly beautiful. God loved them with a love that would not let them go, no matter the cost.

The impact of that story surely was transmitted to the children. It was a reality they lived with every day. Did they live in view of the precious tree of life from which they were now barred? Every day did they look at what sin had cost them? Did Abel grow to hate sin, and, in contrast, did Cain grow to resent God? Do you think it is possible that two brothers, both looking on the same scene, came to two different conclusions?

When the time came for worshipfully making an offering to the Lord, Cain skimped. The context of both the story in Genesis and of the synopsis in Hebrews implies that God's requirements for an acceptable sacrifice were well known. When the writer of Hebrews says that "by faith Abel offered," then the shorthand is meant to communicate that Abel's sacrifice was in direct obedience to God's revealed word. Evidently, Cain knew the same thing Abel knew, but chose not to obey.

I imagine that when Abel killed some of the firstborn of his flock to bring as an offering to the Lord, the blood spilled was precious to him. When he deliberately surrendered by faith a living thing that was valuable to him, necessary to him for food and clothing and shelter, it cost him. He didn't take the easy way out. He didn't try to get by holding on to all he could. He let it all go. He understood the eternal truth that "without the shedding of blood there is no forgiveness" (Hebrews 9:22).

"By faith Abel offered." Without knowing the details of redemption's eternal plan, Abel's obedient sacrifice was looking ahead, previewing and embracing the future event that would provide the substance of which his act was a shadow. He believed that God would indeed accept his offering as a covering for his sins. Because God had declared it so, he believed—evidenced by his obedience—that his offering would restore the relationship that sin had poisoned. Without understanding it, he embraced the promise that he could walk with God and that God had provided a way for intimacy between a sinful man and a holy God. Abel accepted that God loved him and longed for his companionship so much that He made a way to deal with the sins that would break that fellowship. When Abel prepared his offering, the blood that was poured out surely reminded him of the horrible cost of sin and the unfathomable love of God.

IMITATE ABEL

Adam and Eve sinned, and immediately God covered them. Then at some point, we have to assume, He instructed them about offering blood sacrifices to cover sins. Why do you think that from the beginning God prepared a remedy for sin? Among other reasons, it was because He knew that guilt and shame would cripple, hindering His people from becoming what He had designed them to be.

Your enemy, Satan, knows the same thing. He makes good use of guilt and shame to hold God's people back, slow them down, even stop them in their tracks. This is so typical of his ploys that it has earned him a nickname in the kingdom: the accuser of the brethren. When he uses shame and guilt to hinder, it is often cleverly disguised in pious-sounding emotions and thoughts. But however you package it, holding on to guilt and shame denies the power of the Cross.

If God said that the blood of the Lamb provided for your forgiveness and set you free from guilt and shame, then believe it.

> "This is my blood of the covenant, which is poured out for many for the forgiveness of sins."
> —Matthew 26:28

In him we have redemption through his blood, the forgiveness of sins, in accordance with the riches of God's grace that he lavished on us with all wisdom and understanding.
—Ephesians 1:7–8

To him who loves us and has freed us from our sins by his blood.
—Revelation 1:5

Recently I was speaking at a retreat and this topic came up in a live question-and-answer time. A woman, genuinely in grief with tears flowing freely, spoke between sobs: "I just can't forget for a moment that my sins took Jesus to the Cross. I am continually grieved that He had to die for me and that I might as well have pounded the nails." This is an emotion that comes from her great love for Jesus and her realization of the terrible price He paid for her, and it is legitimate up to a point.

Grief over our sins and the conscious awareness that He paid their price is certainly foundational to our salvation. To be reminded of salvation's cost is appropriate. But to live in grief, shamed by your sins, is not.

Imagine that someone you love has gotten herself into severe debt, so severe that she has no way out. Now, imagine that you have the means to pay the debt and give that person a fresh start. Imagine her joy when you tell her that her debt is paid and she is free. Her joy gives you joy. Now, imagine that instead of delighting in her new freedom and living out her new opportunity, she instead is grieved because you had to rescue her. She can't move on in her new life because she is so crippled by shame from the fact that she needed your help. Kind of takes all the fun out of it, right?

God is not surprised at your sin. Because He knew you would sin, He set the Cross in place from the beginning. Jesus is called "the Lamb that was slain from the creation of the world" (Revelation 13:8). As He always does, God prepared the solution before the problem arose. He is always ahead of the curve.

The affront to the Cross is not that you sin. The affront to the Cross, I say, is when we refuse to receive the forgiveness that He paid so high a price for us to have.

Like Abel, believe that when God said His Son's death wipes your slate clean, He was telling the truth. In a later chapter, we will discuss in detail how to close the door to those old, pre-fabricated thoughts that have made themselves at home in you. Right now, begin the inventory of ways that shame and guilt might be hindering you in the race set for you to run.

Do you recognize any ways that your enemy plays on past sins committed by you or against you to keep shame and guilt alive? Can you see how the enemy connives to keep your attention on your perceived failings and hinders you from reaching out to those around you? When we are focused on ourselves and consumed with our own failings, it keeps us from being alert to the needs of others. If Satan can work his plan, holding you hostage to your shame, then he can override God's plan to use you as a vessel through which He actively loves the world. Do you choose to believe God or the accuser of the brethren?

ENOCH

"By faith Enoch was taken from this life, so that he did not experience death; he could not be found, because God had taken him away. For before he was taken, he was commended as one who pleased God. And without faith it is impossible to please God, because anyone who comes to him must believe that he exists and that he rewards those who earnestly seek him" (Hebrews 11:5–6).

"By faith Enoch was taken." Read the original account in Genesis 5. The specific verses that describe Enoch are verses 21–24. But take the time to read the whole chapter. It's one of those genealogy chapters—who begat whom. But the story of Enoch is not complete without it. As you read it, watch the rhythm. "So-and-So lived...and then he died." He lived, and then he died. Over and over, generation after generation. He lived, and then he died. The drumbeat never varies. Until Enoch. Enoch throws everything out of sync. Read it and you'll see what I mean.

Enoch breaks the rhythm. Where everyone else "lived," Enoch "walked with God." Where everyone else "died," Enoch "was no more, because God took him away." The writer of Hebrews makes the claim that before Enoch was taken, he was commended as one who pleased God. And, reasons the writer, no one can please God without faith, so Enoch's walk was a walk of faith.

Paul exhorts us to "keep in step with the Spirit" (Galatians 5:25). Walking is a metaphor for keeping in step with God. Enoch walked with God.

My late husband was very tall. His stride was much longer than mine. When we walked together, I could not match his stride. He would sometimes forget and be far ahead of me, talking to me as if I were right beside him. He had to be intentional about pacing his steps so that I could walk with him instead of behind him. He had to want to walk with me.

When I read that Enoch walked with God, the first thing that amazes me is that it means that God walked with Enoch. God was willing to condescend to calibrate His stride for Enoch's sake—to take into account Enoch's frailty. When Almighty Eternal God took on flesh in Jesus, He showed us in no uncertain terms that He would walk with us.

My sister and I walk together for exercise. When we walk together, we get so caught up in our talking and praying together that the effort and drudgery of walking is forgotten. When Enoch walked with God, though it means that his steps were on the right path, it also means that Enoch was engrossed in the relationship. When Enoch walked with God, his life naturally became pleasing to God—righteous and holy. He didn't have to worry about pleasing God or gods by following a rigid set of religious rules. Caught up in the moment and the joy of God's company, Enoch followed the Ruler.

Let me illustrate how that relationship makes a difference in your walk. In times past in my travels, I had to depend on a map or a set of directions. I was always paying attention to the directions. Counting the miles, watching for the turn, reading the signs. It took all my attention to follow the directions. Now I have a GPS. What a difference! I know that my GPS is doing the watching for me. I know my GPS will tell me when and where to turn, and will get me where I'm going. Now I can enjoy the scenery or the company of passengers. I am freed from the difficult, absorbing job of keeping in step with the directions.

I can give my attention to the needs around me. Enoch, I think, found his walk freeing and exhilarating because he was caught up in the relationship, not the rules.

So intimate was the relationship that when the appointed time came for Enoch to leave earth and enter eternity, his walk just continued. One last step on earth's ground, next step in heaven's vast expanse. Death for Enoch was the natural extension of his life. He just kept walking with God. He received the promise early that came later to the followers of the Christ: "Whoever lives and believes in me will never die" (John 11:26).

IMITATE ENOCH

Your enemy knows that one of the most effective hindrances to your freedom march is to enslave you to a religious system of laws and regulations and expectations. Religion, as opposed to relationship, becomes a grind, a duty, an experience of failure and humiliation. That which God has established for your freedom becomes the very means of your enslavement. Paul says, "I found that the very commandment that was intended to bring life actually brought death" (Romans 7:10).

My friend author Beth Misner came out of a legalistic religious background built on rules. She grew up in a tradition that rejected grace and embraced the idea that only by keeping the Old Testament law—even the ceremonial laws like feasts— could one hope to reach heaven. Coming from that past into a realization of freedom, her joy is contagious. She has such a fresh appreciation for the freedom of a relationship with Christ.

She wrote to me:

> I was raised to believe that my law keeping (or lack thereof) would determine where and how I would spend the rest of eternity. It was such a mixed-up way to live, so marked by guilt and shame and sorrow over attempts to live sin free... [attempts] that only made it a few hours at a time! I was also raised to believe that my actions could disqualify me from the kingdom of God—that I had to earn my way into God's kingdom. I remember, as I was

emerging from this belief system, reading the Bible with fresh eyes and wondering how I could have ever been held captive by such wrong conclusions and misguided interpretations. It really was unbelievable!

Freedom...yes, it means a lot to me and I pray to be used by Jesus to lead many, many others to this freedom...the only true freedom there is anyway, freedom in Christ.

Some of us who know the teaching of freedom and grace still get trapped in types of legalism. Trying to please God, or trying to please parents, or spouses, or peers. Afraid to step out and be different for fear of criticism or rejection. The embedded belief that good boys and girls act a certain way and that only good boys and girls are worthy of love is a weight that holds us back and keeps us from running the race flat-out, unhindered. We lose sight of the relationship, the presence of Christ, and get hijacked by the demands and expectations of others. We miss out on the relationship Enoch must have experienced.

Do you see any legalism in your life? Any ways that rules have replaced relationship in your walk with Christ? Do you recognize any places where fear of losing favor keeps you paralyzed and afraid of risk? Do you identify ways that legalism keeps you self-centered and blinded to the ways that you could be looking outward to the needs of others?

Again, we will address later specifics about how to throw off this hindrance. Right now, just look it in the eye and name it. It's the starting place.

NOAH

"By faith Noah, when warned about things not yet seen, in holy fear built an ark to save his family. By his faith he condemned the world and became heir of the righteousness that comes by faith" (Hebrews 11:7).

"By faith Noah...built." Read his story in Genesis 6–8. Observe the descriptions of the times in which he lived. Only a few generations from Adam and Eve, what has humanity become?

Life Unhindered!

Noah lived in the midst of a perverse people. This is before God called out Abraham and the nation of Israel to be His proving ground. There was no group of people who were living in covenant with God in the midst of the evil. See what happens when humans are left to let their sinful natures flower with no mitigating influence? Noah lived in a time of evil such as has never been again. Look at the language God uses to describe them. "The LORD saw how great man's wickedness on the earth had become, and that every inclination of the thoughts of his heart was only evil all the time" (Genesis 6:5). Pretty strong statements. Pretty grim situation.

In the middle of all that evil there was a man named Noah who walked with God. He was attuned to the voice of God and familiar with the heart of God. Because he was walking with God in an active and dynamic interaction, the evil of his time couldn't penetrate. It was as if he was in the middle of a flood, but was covered with an impenetrable substance and so did not absorb the sea of sin that surrounded him. As if he floated on it, outside it. As if he were an ark, covered with pitch inside and out.

The word used in Genesis 6:14 for *coat* is the same Hebrew word that we translate "atonement." The Hebrew word translated "pitch" in the same verse is from the same root. These words are later used to talk about the blood covering that atones, The literal meaning of *atonement* is "to make one." In the construction of the ark, the pitch covered over the boards and filled in the gaps between, making it one solid whole, and the pitch repelled the water, making it waterproof. When the pitch was applied, it bonded with the wood and became one with it. The pitch could never be removed from the wood. Nothing could penetrate the covering of pitch.

When the blood of the Lamb covers your life, you are reconciled—made one—with God, and your life is protected from the evil with which the world is polluted. The blood of Christ, applied to your life, is fixed permanently. It has altered the construction of your life and you are someone altogether new and different. Nothing can penetrate the covering of the blood.

IMITATE NOAH

We are arks in a sea of evil and sin. We don't have to be removed from the world to be separated from its influence. We can stand firm and strong right smack-dab in the middle of a world of sin. Our enemy tries to hinder us by making the mind-set of the world seem harmless or attractive. Envy, lying, gossiping, anger, selfish ambition, dissension...these habits and attitudes, which mirror the world's ways, can find their way into our lives before we recognize them. He can't get them through the blood covering, but we can open the door. Remember that the ark had a great big door. Later we'll look at how to keep that door closed, locked from the inside.

Some believers feel compelled to withdraw from the world in order to be kept safe from its warping influence. But Jesus prayed just the opposite for us. "My prayer is not that you take them out of the world but that you protect them from the evil one. They are not of the world, even as I am not of it" (John 17:15–16). He sends us into the world as salt and light. We are to wade right in, taking the light right into the darkness.

Knowing that God has provided for our protection, we can go. We can engage our culture and influence those around us, as Jesus demonstrated. Jesus did not keep Himself closed off from the messiness of the world's needs. He waded in and stood waist-deep in humanity's hurts.

Missionary Amy Carmichael exhibited this Jesus-fueled, passionate engagement of the culture. The ripple effects of her brazen, audacious, determined love for the unloved continue to this day. Amy, born into a comfortable life in Ireland, one day had that comfortable life interrupted by a seemingly insignificant event that turned out to be a pivotal moment, leading her into the depths of humanity's pain. She tells the story this way:

It was a dull Sunday morning in a street in Belfast.... My brothers and sisters and I were returning with our mother from church when we met a poor, pathetic old woman who was carrying a heavy bundle. We had never seen such a thing in Presbyterian Belfast on Sunday, and, moved by sudden pity, my brothers and I turned

Life Unhindered!

with her, relieved her of the bundle, took her by her arms as though they had been handles, and helped her along. This meant facing all the respectable people who were, like ourselves, on their way home. It was a horrid moment. We were only two boys and a girl, and not at all exalted Christians. We hated doing it. Crimson all over (at least we felt crimson, souls and body of us) we plodded on, a wet wind blowing us about, and blowing, too, the rags of that poor old woman, till she seemed like a bundle of feathers and we unhappily mixed up with them. But just as we passed a fountain, recently built near the curbstone, this mighty phrase was suddenly flashed as it were through the grey drizzle:

"Gold, silver, precious stones, wood, hay, stubble—every man's work shall be made manifest: for the day shall declare it, because it shall be revealed by fire; and the fire shall try every man's work of what sort it is. If any man's work abide..."

If any man's work abide: I turned to see the voice that spoke with me. The fountain, the muddy street, the people with their politely surprised faces, all this I saw, but saw nothing else. The blinding flash had come and gone; the ordinary was all about us. We went on. I said nothing to anyone, but I knew that something had happened that had changed life's values. Nothing could ever matter again but the things that were eternal.
— Amy Carmichael, *Gold Cord*

Amy became a missionary in India, where, against all convention, she reached out to little girls who had been handed over to the Hindu temples to become temple prostitutes. She rescued thousands and built a village called Dohnavur Village. Amy became mother—"Amma"—to thousands of motherless children and redirected the course of their lives. Extraordinary needs— glossed over or hidden in shadow—will present themselves to the one who fearlessly wades into the muck of sinful humanity, certain of the protective covering of the God who sends.

But be on the alert for Satan's sneak attacks. He wants you either withdrawn from the world, where you will become self-focused and fearful, or he wants you absorbed into the world, where you will be diminished and diluted. Either way, he is able to hinder you and slow you down.

Identify what you see as a danger in your life. Afraid of the world? Or absorbed by the world? Do you fear being available to those in the world who need to know Christ? Or, is your life indistinguishable from the world in its goals and drives?

Discussion

1. How did Abel, Enoch, and Noah live unhindered? Review the potential hindrances that Abel, Enoch, and Noah laid aside.

2. How might each of these hindrances keep believers from experiencing the freedom Christ offers?

3. How might each of these hindrances keep a believer focused on herself? How does this play into the enemy's schemes for keeping us from full freedom?

4. Review the concepts and identify insights that relate to some or all of the four characteristics of fully free people.

   - Be vehicles through which God's Spirit will be unleashed in the world.

   - Be leaders of influence and uncompromised integrity.

   - Be courageous in their calling and engaged in their culture.

   - Be passionate about God as they step out and take risks together with other believers.

CHAPTER 2

God of Our Fathers

In the next grouping in Hebrews 11 we are directed to observe the patriarchs, covering the time from after the Flood to the Exodus from Egypt. These men's lives become the clay from which God begins to sculpt a nation, calling out a man through whom would come a people. This people would become His platform where He would work out His plans for all humanity. Through this nation, He would put Himself on display. Through this people, His Spirit would be unleashed in the world.

ABRAHAM, SCENE ONE

Our attention is directed to Abraham three times. The Holy Spirit spotlights three scenes in the drama of Abraham's walk. Something in each of these specified crisis events gives us a glimpse into how to throw off every hindrance. The writer gives a quick overview, devoid of detail, knowing his audience can and will fill in all the blanks.

> *By faith Abraham, when called to go to a place he would later receive as his inheritance, obeyed and went, even though he did not know where he was going. By faith he made his home in the promised land like a stranger in a foreign country; he lived in tents, as did Isaac and Jacob, who were heirs with him of the same*

promise. For he was looking forward to the city with foundations,
whose architect and builder is God.
  —Hebrews 11:8–10

Read the story in Genesis 12:1–3 and read another version of it
in Acts 7:2–5. Expect to receive some new and fresh thought in
what may be a familiar story to you. Read with anticipation.

Abraham, apparently the youngest of Terah's three sons,
lived with his wife, Sarai, and his extended family along the lush
banks of the Euphrates River, in Ur of the Chaldees. The city
in which Abraham resided was the center of Chaldean moon
worship. The Scripture informs us that Abraham and his family
were idol worshippers. They lived in a land of idol worshippers and "worshiped other gods" (Joshua 24:2). The Scripture
is silent on the details of what set Abraham apart from everyone
else. We don't really know why God singled him out, wooed
his heart, and appointed him father of a nation, and father of
all who by faith would believe in Jesus Christ (Romans 4:16).
I think the Scripture is silent on the matter because it wasn't
about Abraham, it was about God.

We can surmise a little. God's work with Abraham must
have been consistent with His work in the lives of others whom
He called. So, assume that throughout Abraham's life, God
had been doing preparatory work leading to the call—the race
marked out for Abraham to run. When Abraham heard the
call to leave everything behind to press forward to what was
ahead, it was surely not the first time Abraham had heard His
voice. Perhaps Abraham had heard God's voice as he walked
along the banks of the Euphrates, so that when God's promise
included descendants "as the sand of the sea," it might have
immediately brought to mind previous encounters. Or when the
promise included heirs "as the stars in the sky," Abraham may
have remembered experiencing His presence under the bright
stars in the clear night skies of beautiful Mesopotamia.

In any case, God certainly must have spoken in ways
that connected with Abraham's heart. It is only reason-
able to expect that God had led Abraham step by step,
line by line, a little at a time, to the monumental call,

"Lekh lekha" — "Go for yourself" or "Go you forth." It was a very personal call.

God's commands are, in the end, promises. He commands an obedience that will clear the way for His promised provision. Notice the structure of the command and the corresponding structure of the promise. Read the command in Genesis 12:1. "The LORD had said to Abraham, 'Leave your country, your people and your father's household and go to the land I will show you.'"

The command is to leave (1) your country; (2) your people; and (3) your father's household. Do you see how it starts with the remote—your country—and moves progressively to the very personal—your family? The command does not end with what Abraham must leave behind. It commands him to possess and embrace what lies ahead. The command is already a promise: "Let go of what is in your hand right now so that your hand will be ready to grasp what I am about to give."

Author F. B. Meyer puts it this way:

> There is an old Dutch picture of a little child dropping a cherished toy from its hands; and, at first sight, its action seems unintelligible, until, at the corner of the picture, the eye is attracted to a white dove winging its flight toward the emptied outstretched hands. Similarly we are prepared to forego a good deal when once we catch sight of the spiritual acquisitions which beckon to us. And this is the true way to reach consecration and surrender. Do not ever dwell on the *giving-up* side, but on the ***receiving*** side.... There will not be much trouble in getting men to empty their hands of wood, hay, and stubble if they see that there is a chance of filling them with the treasures which gleam from the faces or lives of others, or which call to them from the page of Scripture.
> —*The Way into the Holiest*

The promise is attached to the command. God is not commanding Abraham to make this sacrifice for sacrifice's sake, but to make way for the promise. The call to crucifixion is always to make a way for resurrection.

Note the promise in Genesis 12:2–3. "I will make you into a great nation and I will bless you; I will make your name great, and you will be a blessing. I will bless those who bless you, and whoever curses you I will curse; and all peoples on earth will be blessed through you."

Leave your country	I will make you into a great nation.
Leave your people	I will make your name great — or, I will populate the earth with your name; your name will be borne by a great number of people; I will multiply your name through a new people.
Leave your family	All the peoples on earth will be blessed through you.

For each sacrifice, a restoration. For each crucifixion, a resurrection. When God calls us to courageous risk, He is promising His provision. He is not calling us to risk for risk's sake, but so that through us He can unleash His Spirit in the world.

By the time Abraham heard the call, *"Lekh lekha,"* I think it is likely the voice of the Lord had become familiar to him. Perhaps he had heard and obeyed it before, in smaller things. He had learned by experience that the voice could be trusted. He knew firsthand that losing one thing meant gaining something more. I love the way F. B. Meyer puts it: "(Our spirit) grows by surrender, and waxes strong by sacrifice."

God called Abraham to turn his eyes away from the beautiful, fruitful, vibrant Euphrates and set his path toward the desolate desert. In Abraham's heart, he constructed an altar. There he lay down places, people, and things that he once thought belonged to him by right. He would visit that heart's altar again before his race was finished. The course we travel is marked by altars. We move from one *altared* moment to the next, and at each altar, we are altered. I want to make up a word. Am

I allowed? I want us to use the noun *altar* as a verb. When we are *altared*, we are in the midst of laying ourselves on the altar, and we are being changed—altered—in the experience. When we are *altared*, we are dying to what we thought we owned and surrendering all our expectations. At the same time, we are embracing the promise of provision.

God identified for Abraham some attachments—country, people, family—that would hinder him in the race he was about to run. He had to strip down and lay aside anything that would slow his progress.

Serious racers are always on the lookout for ways to decrease the drag caused by the garments they wear. Specialty clothing exists for the elite racer—running, biking, or swimming. Currently there is some controversy in the world of competitive swimming springing from the idea that suits have now become so high-tech that a person can be beaten in a race, not by skill, but by a suit. One blogger describes the new swimming suit technology this way: "Not only are the materials space-age, the actual cut of the suits is also designed to change the shape of the athlete's body, presumably squashing any sticky-out bits that cause extra drag."

In the race set out for you, be as diligent as those who are running to win a temporal prize. Abraham was willing to shed every encumbrance—anything that would knock even a millisecond off his time in his determined quest for the promise God had set before him. He was the forerunner, showing those who would come behind how to run the race unencumbered. He would be the model for the Apostle Paul, who wrote:

> *Do you not know that in a race all the runners run, but only one gets the prize? Run in such a way as to get the prize. Everyone who competes in the games goes into strict training. They do it to get a crown that will not last; but we do it to get a crown that will last forever. Therefore I do not run like a man running aimlessly; I do not fight like a man beating the air.*
> —1 Corinthians 9:24–26

I press on to take hold of that for which Christ Jesus took hold of me. Brothers, I do not consider myself yet to have taken hold of it. But one thing I do: Forgetting what is behind and straining toward what is ahead, I press on toward the goal to win the prize for which God has called me heavenward in Christ Jesus.
—Philippians 3:12–14

Are you being *altared* right now? Or have you been *altared* in the past? What is being stripped away, squashed, or squeezed?

IMITATE ABRAHAM

God is a pruner. "Every branch that does bear fruit he prunes so that it will be even more fruitful" (John 15:2–3). He cuts away foliage that looks beautiful, but is instead a life-drain. Clearing the way for more fruit. Sometimes the things we get most attached to, the things we are most proud of, are only taking up space where lasting fruit could be growing.

We have a tendency to let exterior things define us and give us our sense of value. Our families, our careers, our possessions, our friends, our accomplishments, our reputations. Not that there is anything wrong or sinful about any of these things, unless they get themselves wrapped around us so that we are captive to them. How will we know if something that is innocuous in itself has become a hindrance to more fruit? When we are forced to let them go. Then we find out how possessed of them we have become.

My friend—I'll call her Kathy—is being pruned. Her husband lost his well-paid position and has been unemployed for almost two years. College degrees, years of experience, great networking system, and still he can't find a job. He earns an hourly wage in a part-time retail job. Their savings are gone, their pride has been pummeled, foreclosure on their beautiful home seems likely. Kathy says, "I had no idea I was so possessed by my possessions and my position. I thought that I thought they were just avenues for serving God. Letting them go has been like undergoing surgery without an anesthetic."

The truth is, Kathy's pruning hurts me. I want God to give some of her foliage back, just for a minute. If my love for

Life Unhindered!

Kathy were the deciding factor, she would be comfortable and coddled and cushy. And she would be missing the amazing—if terrifying—journey of letting go. With each thing that gets pruned away, Kathy becomes more unhindered. Her dependence on God grows deeper, and she is possessed by something new: a promise that He will not leave her or forsake her. A quiet confidence has taken the place of the panic and fear and she is willingly being *altered* right now.

I'll quote F. B. Meyer again, this time from *Abraham or The Obedience of Faith*: "So long as we are quietly at rest amid favorable and undisturbed surroundings, faith sleeps as an undeveloped sinew within us; a thread, a germ, an idea. But when we are pushed out from all these surroundings with nothing but God to look to, then faith grows suddenly into a cable, a monarch oak, a master principle of the life."

Missionary Jim Elliot and four of his co-workers were murdered by Huaorani (Auca) tribesmen in Ecuador in 1956 as they sought to bring the gospel to them. Their martyrdom is an example of how even in the ultimate sacrifice, death, God gives us far greater reward.

Elliot had a burning passion to see this tribe introduced to Jesus Christ, and he pared down his life to only that which would help him accomplish this calling. He wrote, "God, I pray Thee, light these idle sticks of my life and may I burn for Thee. Consume my life, my God, for it is Thine. I seek not a long life, but a full one, like you, Lord Jesus." At the moment of his death, Elliot received the eternal reward of fellowship with his Lord forever.

His murder also opened the hearts of the Huaorani to the ministry of other missionaries, including his wife, Elisabeth, and their young daughter. Today there are numerous Christ followers among this tribe. The defining core of Jim's commitment is best expressed in his own words: "He is no fool who gives what he cannot keep to gain that which he cannot lose."

What is God pruning right now in your life? Can you endure the pain of the pruning if you know it is clearing the way to fruitfulness? Is the pain of being *altered* offset by the promise of being powerful and effective in ministry?

ABRAHAM, SCENE TWO

By faith Abraham, even though he was past age—and Sarah herself was barren—was enabled to become a father because he considered him faithful who had made the promise. And so from this one man, and he as good as dead, came descendants as numerous as the stars in the sky and as countless as the sand on the seashore (Hebrews 11:11–12).

Translators disagree on how this passage should be translated. Some think that it refers to Sarah's faith and some that it refers to Abraham's. Different translations will word it differently. For the purposes of hearing what God is saying, it makes little difference. Either way, the same principle is in evidence. Since Abraham is the life we are focused on right now, let's assume Abraham's faith is the subject.

The hinge phrase in this synopsis is "because he considered him faithful who had made the promise." This is a fact about Abraham that is highlighted in Paul's writings: Abraham believed God.

> *[Abraham] is our father in the sight of God, in whom he believed— the God who gives life to the dead and calls things that are not as though they were. Against all hope, Abraham in faith believed and so became the father of many nations, just as it had been said to him, "So shall your offspring be." Without weakening in his faith, he faced the fact that his body was as good as dead—since he was about a hundred years old—and that Sarah's womb was also dead. Yet he did not waver through unbelief regarding the promise of God, but was strengthened in his faith and gave glory to God, being fully persuaded that God had power to do what he had promised. This is why "it was credited to him as righteousness."*
> —Romans 4:17–22

When Paul wrote these words, he was expounding on Genesis 15:5–6: "'Look up at the heavens and count the stars—if indeed you can count them.' Then he said to him, 'So shall your offspring be.' Abraham believed the LORD, and he credited it to him as righteousness."

Stop now and read Genesis 15:1–6. Read it with your sanctified imagination unfurled. Put yourself in Abraham's shoes. As you read it, see it.

Now look again at how the writer of Hebrews summarizes this event. Notice something about the way the writer of Hebrews constructs this sentence. Abraham "was enabled to become a father." Abraham is not the doer of the action. Rather, he is the object—the one acted upon. In this demonstration of faith, there is nothing for Abraham to do but receive. All the action comes from God. Paul uses the same kind of structure when he says that Abraham "was strengthened in his faith." Abraham is the receiver of the strengthening.

When you read the account in Genesis, you are encountering a high point of both Jewish and Christian theology. The whole grand story from beginning to end turns on this moment when Abraham believed God, and God credited it to him as righteousness. Abraham believed God, so everything can go forward. The promise can be fulfilled. But, observe how Abraham is simply persuaded by living word of God spoken to him in real time. And for the first time, the Scripture states that Abraham believed God.

Abraham believed God. The Hebrew verb suggests that Abraham entrusted himself to God as a child entrusts himself to his parent. God had made promises to Abraham before. Had Abraham not believed until now?

Abraham had believed in the past. He had risked everything on his confidence in God's promise. But before, Abraham had believed God because what God promised was believable. God promised Abraham. Abraham evaluated the promise and said to himself, "Sure. That could happen." God promised Abraham a son. Abraham and Sarai were still in their childbearing years. That's believable. Abraham believed *the promise*.

Now the promise is no longer believable. The promise hinges on a son. Sarai is past the age of childbearing. Now Abraham does something different. He believes *God*. His faith rests in who God is—his shield and his very great reward. God looked on it as righteousness. He credited it to Abraham as if it were righteousness. He dealt with Abraham as if Abraham were righteous.

Abraham shifted his focus from the circumstances and fastened it on the Person who had the power to do what He promised. Faith flooded in. He received. He gave himself up to the living word of the living God and quit trying to evaluate and measure the circumstances to see if there was still a chance that God could come through. He stopped letting his own sense of what should be happening hinder him in his journey of faith. He let God deliver the promise at the appointed time. He received.

IMITATE ABRAHAM REMIX
Are you hindered by the circumstances you find yourself in? Are you so consumed with the events of the moment that you have lost sight of the big picture?

"So we fix our eyes not on what is seen, but on what is unseen. For what is seen is temporary, but what is unseen is eternal" (2 Corinthians 4:18).

God is the big picture. When He is the focal point, then everything else takes on the proper dimensions. We see things in perspective. Big God. Little circumstances.

Abraham could do nothing to hurry the promise. There was no work he could perform that would change the timetable. This reality is echoed in the New Testament in a conversation between Jesus and the following crowds: "Then they asked him, 'What must we do to do the works God requires (i.e., so we can have the food you speak of)?' Jesus answered, 'The work of God is this: to believe in the one he has sent'" (John 6:28–29; parenthetical words added to clarify context.)

Are you waiting for God to come through? Are you feeling overwhelmed by the circumstances that seem to make His promise impossible? Are you trying to find something that you can do to move things along? Something that will put God in motion?

Refocus. Get God in view. Let yourself be strengthened and enabled. Receive. When we are God-focused, we can stand firm. We won't be pushed and shoved by circumstances. We can live lives of courage and integrity. We can let our lives flow in service to others . We don't have to be diminished by events.

Consider missionary William Carey—shoe cobbler turned pastor turned missionary pioneer—who was able to bring the gospel's power to bear in India against seemingly impossible odds simply because he heard a call and would not give up. He stood against the strong discouragement of his peers, who insisted that he should not go. He was undaunted by lack of funds for his undertaking. He held fast when his wife at first refused to accompany him, though she changed her mind at the last minute. He stayed when his five-year-old son died, when his wife had a mental collapse and later passed away, when his second wife passed away. He stayed through years and years of working hard and seeing no fruit. After seven long years of faithful witness, Carey baptized his first convert, Krishna Pal. Over the next decades, he pushed through discouragement and sorrow and disappointment to have an eternal impact on the lives of many.

Circumstances that might have stopped another person only served to drive William Carey deeper into the heart of the Father who would not fail him. Adverse circumstances did not rule Carey. They were not the defining element of his life. He clung to a call, a promise, that would not let him go. It possessed him so thoroughly that the ebb and flow of events could not end his mission.

Carey's influence on India and on missions cannot be overstated. He was the among the country's pioneers in agriculture, horticulture, and education. He was a social reformer who protested the casting of babies into the Ganges as a sacrifice to the gods. And, along with his co-workers, he translated the Word of God, whether fully or in part, into 34 different languages.

Had William Carey's focus not held—had he believed his circumstances instead of believing God—he would have lived a lesser life. A good life, no doubt. A life in which good things were accomplished, I'm sure. But a lesser life.

In later chapters we will look at exactly how to hold your focus on God. Right now, just recognize any situation in which you have shifted your focus from God to your circumstances.

ABRAHAM, SCENE THREE

By faith Abraham, when God tested him, offered Isaac as a sacrifice. He who had received the promises was about to sacrifice his one and only son, even though God had said to him, 'It is through Isaac that your offspring will be reckoned.' Abraham reasoned that God could raise the dead, and figuratively speaking, he did receive Isaac back from death.
—Hebrews 11:17–19

Now Abraham is Abraham. The promised son has been delivered and is about 15 years old when God speaks familiar words to Abraham. "Lekh lekha," He says again, as He had said all those years ago when the call was new and the journey had just begun. "Go you out." Read the story in Genesis 22:1–19.

Hebrew scholars and Jewish people refer to this incident as the *Akeida*, which means "the binding." For them, it is the story of the binding of Isaac. It is a moment of what contemporary Hebrew scholars often call *meta-mitzvah*. *Mitzvah* means "the commandment." Meta-mitzvah is an act of devotion that goes beyond the commandments.

I've been thinking about the binding of Isaac. There are so many elements to the episode, yet Hebrew scholars center it on the binding. When did the binding occur? When 15-year-old Isaac, whose name in Hebrew—Laughter—reflects his father's joy in him, lay down upon the altar, Abraham bound him. It was part of the sacrificial ritual. The act of binding allowed no separation between Isaac and Abraham. Abraham had to touch him and look into his face and hear his voice. How he must have longed to be wrapping his arms around this beloved son rather than tying him to the altar. This moment when the obedience cost him most was indeed meta-mitzvah. It defines the story.

What held Abraham to his task? What kept him from saying, "This is too much!" I believe that what kept Abraham obedient to this command is what I will call the binding of Abraham.

Binding the sacrifice kept the sacrifice from thrashing and resisting and slipping off the altar. Abraham had been *altared* for many years. Waiting for the promised son, living in the promised land as a stranger, giving up the son Ishmael, who was born of his self-effort. Staying still on the altar took all these years for Abraham to learn. Over years and years and through experience after experience, Abraham had learned to stay on the altar. Each step of Abraham's journey bound his heart more firmly to God's until God referred to Abraham as His friend.

Abraham's altar had taught him that God could be trusted. Impossible circumstances were just the stage for God's power. He had learned to stay *altared* and let God work. He'd seen what happened when he crawled down off the altar and took matters into his own hands.

On that most difficult of all days, Abraham's heart was bound to God's so fully that he could lay down his most beloved son because of his unwavering faith in the God who called him. Faith had been learned on the altar.

Faith bound Abraham, as Abraham bound Isaac.

Isaac was God's gift to Abraham. Isaac was the linchpin for everything God had promised Abraham. But Abraham perhaps felt he owned the gift. Maybe he felt too possessive of that which God had given him. By offering up Isaac, Abraham not only freed himself of a hindrance to his walk but he also freed Isaac.

IMITATE ABRAHAM REMIXED AGAIN

Like Abraham, we tend to want to possess those we love. We want to control and manage their lives. We want to control and manage their decisions, their opportunities, and their futures. We want them to be who we want them to be.

These entanglements not only hinder us, but they hinder those we love. By our overpossessive love, we give those we are trying to bless a hindrance that may take a lifetime to overcome. It is the hardest call of all to lay down the people God has put into our lives and called us to love.

Many a parent knows the gripping sorrow of having to lay a child on the altar. When your child is on the altar, you are *altared* and must stay, bound by faith. Otherwise we would rescue, fix, meddle once again.

Many a spouse knows the pain of surrendering a marriage and accepting a spouse for what he or she is, not what you imagined he or she would be. *Altared.* Let the faith that binds you to the altar do the deep work that can only be done on the altar.

Many a believer knows the pain of laying down a long-held expectation and staying *altared* until God has recreated desires and reformed vision.

Remember Abraham's faith: "He reasoned that God could raise the dead." You can take your hands off and let God do what you cannot. You can walk free of the burden of trying to fix someone else, or manage an outcome.

My friend (whom I'll call Judy) has a beautiful young adult daughter. No daughter has ever been more carefully parented, or had more opportunities in life. Judy was an involved and loving, though not indulgent, parent. In her early teen years, Judy's daughter began to exhibit erratic behaviors and finally was diagnosed as bipolar. Judy and her husband have learned everything they can about the condition, have provided their daughter with the best treatment, have been patient and supportive and loving. But the day has come when they have to lay her down. Love her, be there for her, but leave her on God's altar. The process of being *altared* where her precious daughter is concerned has been painful and the temptation to climb down and take over has been almost irresistible at times.

One day recently Judy had a sudden breakthrough. "Suddenly, I'm not sad all the time," she said. She can't explain it, but the hovering sorrow is gone. She is free to walk out her life, and to be supportive of her daughter without getting in God's way. Faith has had to bind her to the altar, but there she is free. The altar is doing its work in her.

Judy could choose to be bound by her daughter's illness, to be consumed with her family's circumstances. But God is *altaring* her. Her life is being poured out in ministry to other troubled young people. As a high school teacher, she has developed a program for truant students in which she can give them encouragement and the push they need to succeed. This program has been so successful that she was recently honored with a significant community commendation for it.

Life Unhindered!

She also teaches a Bible study of young men in prison once a week. They come faithfully because they feel the genuine love she has for them. One evening as she was driving to the prison, she was so grieved and worn down by her situation she told God, "I can't do this. You'll have to take over. I need to know You're there." The night's lesson went exceeding well. At close, she said, "You guys were just great tonight." One of the young men said, "No, you were awesome!" And they gave her a standing ovation. Young men in prison. A standing ovation for a Bible study.

Her *altared* living leaves her free to leave her sorrow in God's hands and pour herself into lives of troubled young people with a holy power that flows from surrender.

Who or what in your life is God calling you to place on the altar, knowing that you will be *altared* in the process? Let your altar do its work in you. Let faith bind you.

When we are engaged in fixing people and managing events, it takes all our energy. We lack the freedom to live courageously and passionately, engaging our culture and displaying Christ to the world.

Discussion

1. Review the three hindrances Abraham laid aside.

2. What did Abraham experience because he was willing to strip down for the race?

3. How would you define our newly minted word *altared*, using your own experiences?

4. Review the concepts and identify insights that relate to some or all the four characteristics of fully free persons.

   - Be vehicles through which God's Spirit will be unleashed in the world.

   - Be leaders of influence and uncompromised integrity.

   - Be courageous in their calling and engaged in their culture.

   - Be passionate about God as they step out and take risks together with other believers.

CHAPTER 3

A Great Nation

The next grouping begins with Moses and follows the nation that was birthed under Moses's leadership. We see the progression of a narrative. God binds His people together into a living organism that is first the nation of Israel, but culminates in the church. We are not scattered individuals, but rather we are a living house, as Peter writes: "You also, like living stones, are being built into a spiritual house" (1 Peter 2:5). Or, the more often discussed metaphor, we are a body, with Jesus as the head. Both pictures show us that God has calculatedly bound us together so that we experience the fullness of our call in relation to each other.

This is so vital to God's plan that it was the principal element of Jesus's high priestly prayer, among the last prayers He prayed before the crucifixion: "So that they may be one as we are one. . . . May they be brought to complete unity to let the world know that you sent me and have loved them even as you have loved me" (John 17:11, 23). He specifies whom He is praying for: "My prayer is not for them alone. I pray also for those who will believe in me through their message" (John 17:20). Read the prayer in John 17 and notice how Jesus prays for the church, His body.

JOCHEBED

"By faith Moses' parents hid him for three months after he was born, because they saw he was no ordinary child, and they were not afraid of the king's edict" (Hebrews 11:23).

Read Exodus 1:29-2:10. As is usually the case, the biblical account is succinct. The drama is left to the imagination. The barest facts speak eloquently.

The Book of Genesis puts high priority on names. Names are important and meaningful and tell a story. Names of places, names of people, names of God. In Exodus, no new names are mentioned until Moses, other than the two Hebrew midwives named Shiphrah and Puah. Moses's parents are "a man of the house of Levi" and "a Levite woman." The cast of characters are "his sister," "the daughter of pharaoh," "a king over Egypt." No names.

After Moses, we begin to learn names again. Between Joseph, the last significant name mentioned, and Moses lay about 400 years. "Joseph died, and all his brothers and all that generation. But the sons of Israel were fruitful and increased greatly, and multiplied, and became exceedingly mighty, so that the land was filled with them" (Exodus 1:6–7 NASB). That is the summary of 400 years.

Why do you suppose the Holy Spirit, as He inspired these recorded words, changed from recording every male name in every generation, and every significant female, to this name-less narrative? Perhaps because He is moving the emphasis off of one individual and transferring it to the nation. Through Moses, He begins to work through a people. Except for the nation of Israel, there is no other need for Moses. Everything about Moses—his birth, his upbringing, his call—is about the Lord's people. God had called Abraham to leave his kindred behind, but He calls Moses to bring his kindred out.

The great nation multiplied in the adversity designed to destroy it. The great nation came together in conditions that had the potential to divide them. The great nation took on a unique identity in a land that might have absorbed them. Everything the enemy meant for evil, God used for good. The years in Egypt were crucible years when the great nation promised to Abraham gestated, until they were born of the water and the blood. I'll explain that statement later. Read on.

From here on in God's unfolding revelation, He does His work through a people. They, collectively, are His platform.

The story of God's people has a preface: the story of Moses. The story of Moses begins with the fearless faith of his mother. When Moses's mother, Jochebed, learned she was pregnant, it seemed that the timing could not be worse. They were slaves in Egypt, in a time when the slaves' condition was the most oppressive: "They made their lives bitter with hard labor in brick and mortar and with all kinds of work in the fields; in all their hard labor the Egyptians used them ruthlessly" (Exodus 1:14). An edict had been given to the whole nation that every Hebrew baby boy was to be thrown into the Nile River (Exodus 1:22). Right at that moment—when it seemed that the worst thing that could happen to a Hebrew mother was to give birth to a son—at that moment, Moses was born.

God's work in our lives is strategic. He is always working according to a carefully engineered timetable and a well laid out plan. Moses's birth was timed perfectly. Just as God had promised Abraham generations before, on the schedule laid out in eternity, Moses was born in Egypt.

> Then the LORD said to him, "Know for certain that your descendants will be strangers in a country not their own, and they will be enslaved and mistreated four hundred years. But I will punish the nation they serve as slaves, and afterward they will come out with great possessions.... In the fourth generation your descendants will come back here."
> —Genesis 15:13–16

Moses's parents, Jochebed and Amram, saw something when they looked at their newborn son. "When she saw the child " she saw past what her eyes were viewing and knew something more. God caused her to lay hold of an idea for saving her son. This was no random, Jochebed-derived idea. It was part of the strategy. Everything about Moses's rescue was part of a judiciously constructed plan that would accomplish God's purpose in God's way and in God's time, down to the naming of the little Hebrew son born to a man of the house of Levi and a Levite woman.

He was named by an Egyptian princess. His adoptive mother explained the naming: "She named him Moses, saying, 'I drew him out of the water'" (Exodus 2:10). She named him *Moshe*, which is the future tense of the word meaning "to draw," according to *Essential Torah* by George Robinson. She named him "He Will Draw." One day, indeed, he would draw his people from the water, when they passed through the sea.

When Jochebed saw her son with her eyes, at the same time she saw a future for him with her heart. Not the death her enemy had proclaimed, but the rescue God had caused her to see. She decided that her enemy's plan for her son's future would not come to pass. She would not base her actions on fear, but on faith.

Did she feel fear? Surely she did. I think when the writer of Hebrews says "they were not afraid of the king's edict," the meaning is that though they may have felt fear, fear did not rule their actions. They did not act in concert with fear, but with faith. Fear did not hinder Jochebed from following the vision God had given her, even though her enemy's voice was loud and intimidating and menacing. Because she was able to latch onto God's promise and ignore the enemy's threats, she could act with courage and integrity in the middle of an ungodly culture. No matter what the cost.

Because Jochebed lived unhindered by fear, Moses's destiny was fulfilled and God's plan for redemption was unleashed. Just a little mom in a sea of moms. One of the nameless actors in the exodus story. Likely no one would have picked her out as the key to Israel's escape from Egypt and central to Israel's possessing the Promised Land. It is amazing how God works unnoticed in the most mundane-seeming situations, through the most obscure people. Abraham of Ur. Jochebed of Egypt. Mary of Nazareth. Unhindered lives facing down fear, one of the enemy's most powerful weapons, to become platforms for God's exploits.

Imitate Jochebed

Have you learned to respond to what your heart sees? Do you live with the eyes of your heart enlightened so that you may see what God is doing? (See Ephesians 1:18.)

You can count on this: Whatever God wants to show you, your enemy wants to obscure and blind you to. Anything the Holy Spirit begins to form in your heart, the enemy will lie to you about. Big lies. Loud lies. Skillful lies.

As soon as your heart begins to be stirred with the Spirit's whisper, "Things don't have to stay on the course they're on now," the enemy goes into action. "A little ark? In the Nile River? Are you kidding?" Or, maybe, "You? Of all people! You?" Or maybe, "Can you imagine how silly you'll look when you fail? You'll embarrass God!" Any of this sound familiar at all?

Jochebed knew what her enemy had declared. She heard him. But as she zeroed in on the vision God had given her, the enemy's huffing and puffing just became background noise. What do you do when a liar lies? You ignore him.

Recognize that if the enemy weren't threatened by what your heart can see—like the pharaoh was threatened by the Israelites—then he wouldn't be doing all he could to distract you and bully you. If what you were about to launch into the Nile were inconsequential, or off the mark, he'd be cheering you on. Start right now building what God has called you to build. Everything starts small. Build it in obscurity and let God decide when to set it afloat. Build in obedience, with no goal but to be obedient to the heavenly vision. (See Acts 26:19). Don't build it to own it; build it to let it go.

In the fall of 1984, Fern Nichols's two oldest children of four were entering junior high school. Her heart was heavy and burdened with concern as she knew they would be facing their greatest test in resisting immoral values, vulgar language, peer pressure, and philosophies that would undermine their faith. She cried out to the Lord asking Him to protect them, to enable them to see clearly the difference between right and wrong, and to help them make good decisions.

The burden to intercede for her boys was overwhelming. She asked God to give her another mom who felt the same burden and who would be willing to pray with her concerning their children and their school. God heard the cry of her heart and led her to another mom who shared her burden. Others were invited to come, and they began meeting the following week for prayer, giving their burdens over to the God who hears.

This was the beginning of Moms In Touch International—moms in touch with God, their children, their schools, and one another through prayer. Today, there are Moms In Touch groups in every state of the United States, and representatives in more than 120 countries around the world.

Ignore the enemy's lies and listen closely to the call. Courage!

MOSES

> *By faith Moses, when he had grown up, refused to be known as the son of Pharaoh's daughter. He chose to be mistreated along with the people of God rather than to enjoy the pleasures of sin for a short time. He regarded disgrace for the sake of Christ as of greater value than the treasures of Egypt, because he was looking ahead to his reward. By faith he left Egypt, not fearing the king's anger; he persevered because he saw him who is invisible."*
> —Hebrews 11:24–27

The writer summarizes a progressive decision on Moses's part. It seems to me that this decision had three crisis moments that led to decisions, each more binding than the one before. The writer has wrapped them all up into one declaration that Moses chose the people of God instead of the riches of Egypt. Under what circumstances did Moses choose to identify with his own people in place of Egypt?

The first time he chose his people over Egypt is described by Stephen in the Book of Acts this way:

> *"Pharaoh's daughter took him and brought him up as her own son. Moses was educated in all the wisdom of the Egyptians and was powerful in speech and action. When Moses was forty years old, he*

decided to visit his fellow Israelites. He saw one of them being mis-
treated by an Egyptian, so he went to his defense and avenged him
by killing the Egyptian. Moses thought that his own people would
realize that God was using him to rescue them, but they did not."
—Acts 7:21–26

Read the original account in Exodus 2:11–15.

Moses chooses for the first time to identify himself with his people by taking their side against an Egyptian. From Stephen's description, it seems that Moses thought of this as a first blow that would begin the process of freeing his people. "Moses thought that his own people would realize that God was using him to rescue them," Stephen said.

The second stage of his choice comes when he chooses to flee Egypt as a criminal, whose crime was to defend an Israelite, instead of reconciling with the pharaoh and reestablishing his position in Egypt. First-century philosopher Philo suggests in his *Works* that the pharaoh was angry, not because Moses had killed a man, but because his grandson disagreed with him on the subject of the Israelites. This act was a public repudiation of the pharaoh's choices. It is likely Moses was held in high regard and could have won the king's favor back had he wanted to try. Instead he chooses to leave his privileged life and to be known as one who had tried to defend the despised Hebrew slaves.

The final stage of his choice, that solidified it for all time, comes when he leads the Israelites out of Egypt, freeing them from the hand of their oppressors, the Egyptians.

These three crises are collapsed into one sentence: "By faith Moses, when he had grown up, refused to be known as the son of Pharaoh's daughter. He chose to be mistreated along with the people of God rather than to enjoy the pleasures of sin for a short time."

He looked at the riches, the delicacies, the ease, the abundance of Egypt—all his by right—compared them to the misery of his kinsmen, and chose the misery over the privilege. Why? Because he saw something beyond what his eyes viewed. Like his mother, he looked at the situation that was and saw what God promised would be. "He regarded disgrace for the sake of Christ as of greater value than the treasures of Egypt, because *he was looking ahead* to his reward" (emphasis mine). He looked at the glitter of Egypt and it paled in comparison to the glory of God.

In the final stages of his choice, he again mirrored his mother: "By faith he left Egypt, *not fearing the king's anger*" (emphasis mine). He looked at situations with the eyes of his heart and fastened his gaze, not on what "is seen, but on what is unseen. For what is seen is temporary, but what is unseen is eternal" (2 Corinthians 4:18).

He was willing to risk the status quo. He was willing to let go of his position. He was willing to lay aside his reputation. He was willing to offend power for the sake of Christ. He was not hindered by fear of the king's anger, or by fear of the opinions of others.

Unhindered by misplaced attachments, Moses could live in response to God, not in response to others. He could engage his culture and lead courageously because he was living unhindered.

IMITATE MOSES

My friend Rich had a promising career in an international Fortune 500 company. In his late thirties, he had just been promoted to a position few people his age had attained. His wife and children were proud of him. He earned a hefty salary and had numerous perks that came with the stature he had acquired. But shortly after his promotion, he realized that his company expected him to do something illegal. It wasn't anything big. Not like he'd be arrested for it. And he knew that it was common practice in the industry. Everybody did it, he kept telling himself. Still, he couldn't escape the Holy Spirit's conviction.

He knew that by addressing this, he would sabotage a career that had been on the rise. They wouldn't immediately fire him, but they would know he wasn't a company man and he would begin a career slide. People he had worked with and cared about would turn against him.

With the full support of his wife, and the prayer support of his prayer group, he let his superiors know that he could not participate. They slapped him on the back and said, "No problem." It wasn't long before he was laid off at the first opportunity.

The timing was terrible. The economy was in a slump and hiring was at a standstill. His previous achievements made it even harder to get a job because he was overqualified for most open positions.

Out of options, he went back to school and became a high school teacher and football coach. He found that he loved working with high school students and his work had meaning every day. No more big fancy houses and cars. No more company trips. No longer envied and admired for his incredible success. Just the joy of touching young lives and making a difference.

This story happened almost twenty years ago, so I called Rich and his wife, Amanda, to see how twenty years had colored the picture.

"Wouldn't go back for anything," says Rich. "I don't make the money I thought I would when I was younger, but I make enough. And enough is enough. That's one of the best gifts of all—to know that enough is enough."

Do you find yourself hindered by an attachment to things or people or position in a way that keeps you from being free to live with complete integrity? What is it that you fear losing? Does that feel like living unhindered? If you are surrounded by your Egypt and have let your Egypt get a foothold in your heart, then you are not free to go when God says go.

MOSES AND THE PASSOVER

"By faith he kept the Passover and the sprinkling of blood, so that the destroyer of the firstborn would not touch the firstborn of Israel. By faith the people passed through the Red Sea as on dry land; but when the Egyptians tried to do so, they were drowned" (Hebrews 11:28–29).

When the writer of Hebrews reports that Moses, and with him Israel, "kept the Passover and the sprinkling of blood," he means for Passover to stand for the miraculous series of ten plagues culminating in the death of the firstborn sons. By means of these escalating plagues, God had displayed His power over Egypt, the pharaoh, the gods of Egypt, and all of nature. He had touched every area of community life and personal life. Yet none of the plagues affected the Israelites. The land of Goshen, where the pharaoh had sequestered them, was spared every plague.

Until the tenth plague they didn't have to do anything to secure their own protection. With the tenth, most terrible plague came a command. God instituted a sacred rite that portrays in visible form an invisible truth. This command to eat a Passover meal was a command to the nation rather than to an individual. Each aspect of the Passover ritual is rich in imagery, cementing this night in the national consciousness and foretelling the story of the Lamb of God and eternal redemption. In the moment, the imagery was hazy, but it would become clearer in retrospect and would be made perfectly clear when the Redeemer Greater than Moses (as Jews call the Messiah) appeared. Read about it in Exodus 12:1–28.

For our purposes, let's direct our attention to the blood of the lamb. The passage in Hebrews seems to invite us there. The first Passover is observed at a moment of high drama. Can you imagine the emotional atmosphere among the Israelites? They may have been skeptical when Moses first appeared to tell them that he had come to set them free, but now they had seen the amazing proofs of God's power on their behalf. They had begun to believe that salvation was near. No living Israelite knew anything except slavery. They had heard the stories of the glory days of their forefather Joseph and the generation that experienced the favor of the ruler. They knew the nation's sojourn into Egypt was not to have been permanent and that there was a land that belonged to them. But they only knew all this as stories, long ago and far away. Now freedom stood in view.

Through the plagues, the people who for 400 years had been singled out for harsh labor and savage beatings by their oppressors were now singled out to be protected and cherished by their God. Now their God was about to give them a tangible sign of His love and protection: the blood of the lamb.

"Then they are to take some of the blood and put it on the sides and tops of the doorframes of the houses where they eat the lambs.... The blood will be a sign for you on the houses where you are; and when I see the blood, I will pass over you. No destructive plague will touch you when I strike Egypt" (Exodus 12:7, 13).

This time, to be under the protection of God, something is required of them. They must follow the instructions for the Passover event, concluding with the meal, prepared and eaten according to the Lord's directions. The central component of all the elements and all the instructions was the blood of the lamb. They were to pour out the blood, dip hyssop into it, and smear it over their doorposts—on each side and over the top, perhaps hinting at the cross that would someday be soaked with the blood of the Lamb of God. God proclaimed the blood's power to protect: "When the LORD goes through the land to strike down the Egyptians, he will see the blood on the top and sides of the doorframe and will pass over that doorway, and *he will not permit the destroyer to enter your houses and strike you down*" (Exodus 12:23, emphasis mine).

When the tenth and most devastating plague came—when the angel of death came to strike every firstborn in Egypt—those under the blood would be spared. "When I see the blood, I will pass over you," God promised. Not just any blood, but blood obtained according to God's detailed plan. The blood turned away death, and secured life for those safely under its protection. On the night of the Passover, a group of slaves became a nation. The nation of Israel was born of blood.

THROUGH THE SEA

They were to eat the Passover meal quickly, ready to leave at a moment's notice. "This is how you are to eat it: with your cloak tucked into your belt, your sandals on your feet and your staff in your hand. Eat it in haste; it is the LORD's Passover" (Exodus 12:11). When the Lord's command came to move out, they were not to be hindered by their old lives. They were to be on their feet, packed and dressed for the journey, ready to obey at a moment's notice. They were to be uncluttered—free to leave what lay behind and reach forward to what lay ahead. Free to grab hold of that for which God had grabbed hold of them.

> *I press on to take hold of that for which Christ Jesus took hold of me. Brothers, I do not consider myself yet to have taken hold of it. But one thing I do: Forgetting what is behind and straining toward*

what is ahead, I press on toward the goal to win the prize for which
God has called me heavenward in Christ Jesus.
—Philippians 3:12–14

The call came in the middle of the night. Stop now and read it in Exodus 12:31–34. Before this, Moses had been demanding that pharaoh let his people go; now pharaoh begged him to take his people out. From one moment to the next, everything can change. Be ready.

The people of God—the great nation—as many as 2 million strong, along with their livestock and the gold and silver they collected from the Egyptians, left Egypt as one. The Lord led them on a roundabout route, landing them at the edge of the Red Sea. Meanwhile, the pharaoh had a change of heart. "When the king of Egypt was told that the people had fled, Pharaoh and his officials changed their minds about them and said, 'What have we done? We have let the Israelites go' and have lost their services!'" (Exodus 14:5). The people who once served the pharaoh's agenda will now be free to serve the Lord.

Notice how the people could have been hindered by their ties to their old life. Even those things they hoped to escape had the potential to keep them bound.

They said to Moses, "Was it because there were no graves in Egypt that you brought us to the desert to die? What have you done to us by bringing us out of Egypt? Didn't we say to you in Egypt, 'Leave us alone; let us serve the Egyptians'? It would have been better for us to serve the Egyptians than to die in the desert!" (Exodus 14:11–12).

The Lord was determined to set them free. He had provision in place and a plan ready for how to break their attachments to the life they knew so they could embrace something new.

> *This is what the LORD says—*
>   *he who made a way through the sea,*
>   *a path through the mighty waters,*
> *who drew out the chariots and horses,*
>   *the army and reinforcements together,*
> *and they lay there, never to rise again,*

extinguished, snuffed out like a wick:
"Forget the former things;
do not dwell on the past.
See, I am doing a new thing!
Now it springs up; do you not perceive it?
I am making a way in the desert
and streams in the wasteland."
—Isaiah 43:16–19

Author Sharon Norris Elliott, in her book *Living a Milk & Honey Life*, makes the observation that there is a difference between adapting to your situation and adopting it. The Hebrews had made themselves at home in Egypt. They thought they wanted to be free, but when freedom came to claim them, they looked back longingly at their slavery.

In the desert the whole community grumbled against Moses and Aaron. The Israelites said to them, "If only we had died by the LORD's hand in Egypt! There we sat around pots of meat and ate all the food we wanted, but you have brought us out into this desert to starve this entire assembly to death" (Exodus 16:2–3).

They knew how to be slaves, but they had not yet learned how to be free. It took one night for God to get His people out of Egypt, but it took 40 years for God to get Egypt out of His people. God would not let them be hindered by the memories that tied them to their past. They could not enter the land He promised them until the generation of flesh that kept them tied to Egypt had all died. (See Numbers 32:11–13.) When the last ties to their old life were gone, they entered the abundance of the promise God had made. No longer weighted down by the past, they could live unhindered.

The Hebrew word translated spirit, wind, or breath is *ruach*. As in the Creation, when the *Ruach* of God hovered over the waters, so on the night of deliverance the Lord caused a strong *ruach* to blow over the sea. As in creation, the *Ruach*'s action brought forth a new beginning. The nation of Israel was born through water.

The blood of the Passover lamb and the water of the sea and the wind were the elements that marked the birth of the great nation. John uses this imagery when he writes:

> *This is the one who came by water and blood—Jesus Christ. He did not come by water only, but by water and blood. And it is the Spirit who testifies, because the Spirit is the truth. For there are three that testify: the Spirit, the water and the blood; and the three are in agreement.*
> —1 John 5:6–9

What are the water, the blood, and the Spirit in agreement about? Read 1 John 2:6–12. This threefold display verifies that God has given us life. He has brought us out of death and into life. With His people as His platform, He started the full-blown plan of redemption. He portrayed the great drama that would one day set us free. But, like the Israelites, we will have to let go of that which binds us to our old lives if we want to fully experience the freedom and fullness God has available.

TIES THAT BIND

How are you tied to your old life? Unforgiveness, maybe? Do you realize that by holding on to a grudge, you are keeping yourself bound to your offender? You are allowing that offender to have power over you, drawing you back into the memory of a past hurt to experience it over and over again.

Are you tied to your old life by habits or attitudes that had their origins in your Egypt? Maybe their origins are generations old, passed down from one generation to the next.

God has made provision for your freedom. He is doing a new thing. The Wind is blowing over the waters, and a miraculous, unexpected route to freedom is right there waiting for you to set foot on the path. Just put one foot in front of the other, one step leads to the next. You do not have to be hindered by your past. In later chapters, we will look at how to access the provision God has already made for your freedom. Right now, just begin to notice where you are hindered by ties to your old life.

Let me illustrate how we need not be tied to our past. How our freedom can even become the catalyst for setting others free too. Born a slave, Harriet Tubman experienced all the horrors and indignities of her position. But in the midst of her slavery, she learned to be free. She developed a deep faith in God, relying on Him for provision and leaning on Him for strength. Her slavery did not enslave her. Eventually, Tubman escaped and made her way to safety. She was no longer a slave, but her own emancipation was not the end of her quest. Tubman was compelled to set others free.

She chose God's call over bitterness. God appointed her to risk everything to rescue her people still in slavery, and that assignment consumed her as she became a conductor on the Underground Railroad transporting slaves out of the South. Known as the "Moses" of her people, she laid aside the safety she had found as a free person and headed back into her Egypt to set others free. Unhindered by an attachment to her own ease and comfort, Tubman chose instead to alleviate the suffering of the people to whom God sent her. Her heart was uncluttered and open so that when God said to go, she went.

JERICHO'S WALLS

"By faith the walls of Jericho fell, after the people had marched around them for seven days" (Hebrews 11:30).

The writer makes a 40-year leap. Forty years earlier, the newborn nation had found themselves with possibilities and choices and freedom they had not known in their lifetime and did not expect to see. One day, everything was just as it had been for 400 years, and the next day Moses came out of the desert with all kinds of wild ideas and extraordinary promises. Life as they knew it began to morph into something unrecognizable. For a period of perhaps eight to ten months, Moses engaged in a showdown with the pharaoh. Their hopes were raised, then dashed over and over. Then, there they were. The victory won, the enemy defeated. Happily ever after. For a day or so.

When the writer of Hebrews jumps over the 40 years of desert time, he knows his readers get the picture. They know that those 40 years were full of stories about a patient, loving

God teaching His people how to rely on Him. His presence never left them. He was always there, represented to their eyes as a pillar of fire by day and a pillar of cloud by night.

Skip ahead to a very early event in the Promised Land. Joshua is their leader now. Moses is dead. They had just crossed over the Jordan by God's miraculous power (Joshua 3:7–17). Then, all the males who were of age were circumcised as soon as they entered the land (Joshua 5:2–9). Water and blood marked their entering into Canaan, just as it had marked their going out of Egypt. The same kind of faith that brought them out of Egypt, now brought them into Canaan.

Then they kept the Passover for the first time. The instruction had been to keep the Passover every year once they entered the land. On the day after they kept the Passover for the first time, they graduated from eating manna to eating the produce of the land of Canaan. No more baby food. No more hand-to-mouth living. Now they had entered the land of abundant living.

The day after the Passover, that very day, they ate some of the produce of the land: unleavened bread and roasted grain. The manna stopped the day after they ate this food from the land; there was no longer any manna for the Israelites, but that year they ate of the produce of Canaan (Joshua 5:11–12).

Forty years earlier, when they first stood on the far side of the Red Sea, they were no longer slaves, but they were not quite free. When they stood on the far side of the Jordan, feet planted on the promised ground, they were free. They began to live like free people. "Then the LORD said to Joshua, 'Today I have rolled away the reproach of Egypt from you'" (Joshua 5:9).

Now they are in the land that God had promised generations before. The land of Canaan, whose boundaries God had marked out and shown to Abraham. But all was not hearts and flowers. They had to take the land. The land was populated. It wasn't just sitting empty waiting for the Israelites. It had been populated for many generations. There were cities and trading routes and industry and cultivated fields. It was this very fact that had scared the previous generation and kept them from receiving God's promise and left them wandering in the wilderness. Read the story in Numbers 13:1–33. It didn't look to them like *their* land. It looked like it already belonged to someone else. Someone else big.

Before they could advance into the land, they had to capture the walled and fortified city of Jericho. It was protected by an impenetrable wall and all the gates were bolted and locked because of their fear of the Israelites. God gave Joshua careful instructions about how to fight this battle, and the instructions were certainly not like everybody else does it.

> Then the LORD said to Joshua, "See, I have delivered Jericho into your hands, along with its king and its fighting men. March around the city once with all the armed men. Do this for six days. Have seven priests carry trumpets of rams' horns in front of the ark. On the seventh day, march around the city seven times, with the priests blowing the trumpets. When you hear them sound a long blast on the trumpets, have all the people give a loud shout; then the wall of the city will collapse and the people will go up, every man straight in."
> —Joshua 6:2–5

The fighting-age men of the Israelites had gained experience in battle during their wilderness journey. They knew how to defeat an enemy on the battlefield. But the instructions God gave for this battle did not rely on their experience or their skill with weapons. This plan called for them to hold back. They had to rein in their impulse to storm the gates. They had to go against the tried and true ways of winning battles. God, in essence, said to them: "Do what I say, and no more. Don't try to call the shots. Don't lean on your own understanding. Acknowledge Me and I will lead you straight to victory."

I have to imagine that for many Hebrew warriors, all the marching and ram's horn blowing felt pretty silly. Surely some of them questioned the wisdom of the plan. They must have felt vulnerable and exposed to the enemy. I can imagine one of these battle-tested warriors telling his story later and saying something like, "The hardest thing I've ever done is not do what I've always done."

But they did what the Lord had commanded. They held back. They marched in circles. When the ram's horn blew, they gave a loud shout. And God gave the victory as He promised He would.

They were not hindered by their own personal opinions. They were free to learn a new way. They were free to let the Lord lead them instead of being led by old habits and patterns. They were free to hold back and let the Lord do what only He can do.

Have you ever noticed that it feels very risky to hold back? Do you feel unsettled when your ways and opinions have to be set aside and brand-new, perhaps untested, methods and ideas take their place? We have to remember that God is telling His story through His people. The story is not all about you. He calls us to risk in company with other believers. You are not on your own. You march with an army under His command.

YOUR JERICHO

Have you ever been hindered by your need to do things the way you think they need to be done? Are you trapped by hardened opinions that leave little room for new approaches? Have you found yourself missing out on exciting relationships, or opportunities, or faith adventures because you refuse to let God do new things new ways?

Maybe you've been ramming the walls of a Jericho with all your might. Here stands some land God wants you to occupy — a promise He wants you to possess. And you've been trying! You've been doing all the things you think you are supposed to do. God is saying, "Hold back, let Me handle it."

It takes passion for God's purposes to have the courage and integrity to stand back and let God do the work in and through ourselves and others. It goes against our instincts. Keeping a focus on God through prayer, praise, and obedience is *not* passive. Sometimes it feels passive because we're used to wearing ourselves out trying to get God's will imposed on a situation. But sometimes He says, "I've got a new way. Follow Me, not tradition."

THE PLATFORM

The writer of Hebrews lists other examples. The Bible is filled with examples. God's people are His platform — His stage. He reveals who He is by what He does in their lives. These examples listed in Hebrews 11 are noted as people whose lives illustrated how faith looks in action and showed us how to throw off every hindrance so that we can run the race with endurance. Look around you. God is telling His story everywhere you look. God is telling His story in you and in the lives of others.

When you read the Scripture, look for God's platform. Look deeper than the words on the page and the scenes the Bible records. Feel free to enter into the story and imagine. Look for the ways God worked to demonstrate unhindered living. Notice what unhindered living produces in the world. Life instead of death; freedom instead of slavery; faith instead of dead tradition.

As you live your own life, be aware that you are God's platform. Every moment of every day, He is telling His story in you, through your life. Every morning when you wake up, first thing, say, "Here I am. Tell Your story in me today."

Be sure to entwine your life with other believers in small groups and prayer partnerships. This is how you see God telling His story in the lives of others. He wants you to have front row seats for His platform in the lives of others.

Discussion

1. Read Jesus's prayer in John 17 and discuss what we see about His heart for the church and the importance of unity.

2. Why does God call us into community with one another?

3. Discuss the hindrances left behind by Jochebed, Moses, and the newborn nation of Israel.

4. Review the concepts and identify insights that relate to some or all of the four characteristics of a fully free people.

   - Be vehicles through which God's Spirit will be unleashed in the world.

   - Be leaders of influence and uncompromised integrity.

   - Be courageous in their calling and engaged in their culture.

   - Be passionate about God as they step out and take risks together with other believers.

Let us throw off everything that hinders and the sin that so easily entangles...

Key 2
His Provision

CHAPTER 4

Untangling

Now that we have looked at many of the examples laid out in Hebrews 11, let's transition to Hebrews 12:1. "Therefore, since we are surrounded by such a great cloud of witnesses, let us throw off everything that hinders and the sin that so easily entangles."

"Therefore" introduces the sentence, clearly pointing us to a continuity of thought. What the writer is about to say builds upon what he has just finished saying. "Since we are surrounded by such a great cloud of witnesses...." Everywhere we look, we can find a witness to the faithfulness of God. God has used their lives as His platform and put Himself on display through them. They stand as witness to Him and proof of His power.

"A *great cloud* of witnesses." In Hebrew culture there are themes and symbols that are immediately recognizable to those attuned to them. "Cloud" is a symbol of the presence of God. The Lord led them for 40 years through the wilderness in a cloud by day. When the presence of God rested over the tabernacle, it was in the form of a cloud. In the wilderness, the cloud of God's presence never left them. The cloud was His presence in a visible form.

We are surrounded by a great cloud of witnesses. God has made Himself visible through their lives. When we observe the collection of witnesses, we are observing the manifested presence of God. Proof of His faithfulness is on display when we study the witnesses. We are observing these who witness to the faithfulness and power of God so that we can learn from them and follow their example. Like them, let us throw off everything that hinders. The word translated "hinders" in this sentence is a Greek word meaning a weight, a burden, an impediment. It is something extraneous that can be shed. It is something that slows our progress.

The next phrase is "and the sin that so easily entangles." This phrase may imply "the sin that entangles" and "the weight that hinders" are two separate things, both of which must be removed. However, it is equally possible that the two phrases are saying the same thing. It is a common Hebrew device to say the same thing twice, in two different phrases. It emphasizes the importance of the thought, and adds further clarity to it. *The Complete Jewish Bible* translates it this way: "So then, since we are surrounded by such a great cloud of witnesses, let us, too, put aside every impediment—that is, the sin which easily hampers our forward movement."

When we have a hindrance in our lives, it is because the active power of sin all around us has found a way to trip us up. Because there is an active spiritual enemy operating in the world, we are susceptible to believing lies that turn into beliefs that become attitudes and actions that weigh us down and slow our progress. The enemy's lies "entangle" us. Do you see the picture? They get wrapped around our ankles, slow us down, and cause us to stumble. We get caught up in them and can't seem to break free. Every thought, attitude, belief, or action that contradicts God's revealed truth is the result of sin. "Everything that does not come from faith is sin" (Romans 14:23).

God wants us free of sin. Untangled. Sin diminishes us and slows our walk and stunts our growth. God wants us to experience the full freedom He has for us. His great love for us is the foundation of His call to walk in freedom. "It is for freedom that Christ has set us free" (Galatians 5:1). Do you see? He has paid the highest price for your freedom *because He wants you to be free*.

His goal is not to scold you or shame you or condemn you, but to free you.

The writer of Hebrews makes this statement a command, "Let us throw off everything that hinders and the sin that so easily entangles." God never commands us to do something for which He has not made full provision.

"His divine power has given us everything we need for life and godliness through our knowledge of him who called us by his own glory and goodness. Through these he has given us his very great and precious promises, so that through them you may participate in the divine nature and escape the corruption in the world caused by evil desires" (2 Peter 1:3–4).

You can consider every command a promise. What He requires, He provides. If He commands, then that is the assurance that what He commands is possible through Him. Every command He gives is meant to set us free. There is a difference between following a strict set of rules of behavior and following the voice of the One who loves us completely and has only our good in mind.

To recap: Because He loves us and wants us to live in His abundance, He calls on us to lay aside those habits, attitudes, and beliefs that are tripping us up in the journey. The very fact that He gives this command tells us that He has provided a way for us to throw off those very habits, attitudes, and beliefs. He died to set us free and He wants us to be free. He is fully invested in seeing us fully free. His battle cry is this: freedom!

This freedom is demonstrated in our service to others. The more freedom you have, the more freely you will serve. "Freely you have received, freely give" (Matthew 10:8).

Jesus's walk on earth was God's platform for how freedom looks. What did Jesus say about His freedom?

"You know that the rulers of the Gentiles lord it over them, and their high officials exercise authority over them. Not so with you. Instead, whoever wants to become great among you must be your servant, and whoever wants to be first must be your slave—just as the Son of Man did not come to be served, but to serve, and to give his life as a ransom for many."
— Matthew 20:25–28

Every Hindrance

Everything that slows our journey or stops our forward momentum is a sin. I have a little concern as we start talking about sin, and I want to just address it with you before we go any further. Some people take sin too lightly, but I don't think those people are reading this book. I think there is a good chance that many readers have a definition of the word *sin* that comes preloaded with condemnation and punishment and shame and guilt. This means that every time I use the word *sin* all those emotions tied to it are going to surface. When we identify weights and hindrances that, at their core, are sin, then you are going to feel discouraged and ashamed and condemned.

God hates sin. No question. If you want to know how much God hates sin, then look at the Cross. God hates sin because God loves you. If you want to know how much God loves you, then look at the Cross.

Sin can be defined as anything that works against your freedom. Because God loves you and is your Protector and Defender, He works in your life to free you of sin.

Now, when the Holy Spirit convicts you of sin, it is because He is calling you to freedom. He convicts in love, not anger. Like a surgeon, He only wounds to heal. You don't have to hide from His heart-searching love in fear of feeling His anger.

Liar, Liar

Every sin—whatever its form—is based in a lie that we believe. Remember that every single thing God wants you to know, Satan wants you to doubt. Satan is a skilled, brilliant liar. Have you ever known a good liar? I mean a really, really good liar? When a good liar lies, what does it sound like? It sounds like the truth. It's convincing. It's bold. It can seem to make more sense than the truth.

His lies have stayed the same since the beginning. He sticks with what works. His lies have had such effect that aspects of them have worked their way deep into our lives. They have managed to soak in like a stain on fabric—right down to the warp and woof of our minds. They are the root of habits, attitudes, and behaviors that hinder us in our journey.

Look at this statement Jesus made: "I tell you the truth, everyone who sins is a slave to sin" (John 8:34–35). I think the logic behind that statement goes like this: We would never sin freely. If we saw things as they are and knew the reality behind the appearance, we would never choose to sin. Sin doesn't make sense. If we could see as God sees, we would not freely choose sin. So, when we sin, we are not acting freely; we are already acting as a slave to the sin that has infiltrated our core.

Let me clarify. I don't mean that we don't make our own choices and have responsibility for them. I mean that if we were fully free with no hindrances that need to be laid aside and no influence from the old script Satan wrote with his lies, we would never choose to sin. It wouldn't make sense. The first sin occurred when Adam and Eve believed Satan's evaluation instead of God's. They only chose to sin because they looked at the appearance of things, and it blinded them to the truth. Had they kept the truth in focus, sin would not have made sense.

Now, let's see what else Jesus had to say in that conversation. "To the Jews who had believed him, Jesus said, 'If you hold to my teaching, you are really my disciples. Then you will know the truth, and the truth will set you free'" (John 8:31–32).

The word translated "hold to" means to dwell or remain or abide; to be in a fixed place. It is the same word used in John 15:5 and 7: "If a man *remains* in me and I in him, he will bear much fruit.... If you *remain* in me and my words *remain* in you, ask whatever you wish, and it will be given you" (emphasis mine). Jesus says that the one who lives in His teaching—who does His teaching—is truly His disciple. When we truly see reality from God's perspective, we won't be tripped up by a distorted view. When we clearly know the truth of any given situation, we will not sin. The truth will make us free.

Let me clarify what I mean. There's knowing—mentally accepting something—and then there's knowing. There are many things that we know, and even believe, but in some cases these truths just haven't put down deep roots for some reason. Here I'm talking about the latter type of knowing—knowledge that is part of you, that has nested in your heart, that defines your desires and directs your actions. For example, if you looked out your door and saw a wild animal headed for you, growling and salivating and obviously on the hunt, would you run outside and greet it? No! It wouldn't make sense. You know not to go outside. Likewise, any time we are seeing sin as God sees it, continuing in it will not make sense. When you know the truth, the truth will make you free.

As a shopper, I have often been fooled by appearance and packaging. I have too often bought something because the packaging was big and bright and shiny and made lovely promises. When I brought it home and opened it up, the contents were something altogether different. Jesus says that when we are learning from Him, He will teach us how to recognize the packaging and distinguish it from the contents—the reality.

In the Book of Romans, Paul described humanity's decline into sin like this: "They exchanged the truth of God for a lie" (Romans 1:25). Where the truth belongs, a lie stands instead. That is our natural state. When we encounter and accept Christ, He begins to progressively replace lies with truth. It's all about lies and truth.

The nature of these lies is such that they are embedded in our makeup. They have to be exposed, uprooted, radiated, surgically removed. They hide and often disguise themselves. They have tentacles that spread to many locations, so just one lie can affect many areas of your life.

These lies don't take root in us simply by hearing them. We have experiences, stored as memories, that have driven home the lie and made it believable. Once implanted, these lies are reinforced until they become our version of reality.

So True

God has made full provision for combating Satan's lies in our lives. From the moment you enter that personal relationship with Jesus, He begins a restoration process. He begins to restore your personality to its intended purpose—to be the place where His glory dwells. To be His platform. Let's assume your human personality consists of your mind, will, and emotions. Your personality is where Satan's lies have done their damage. Of course, if God wants your personality to be a reflection of His glory, then be assured Satan wants to pollute it as much as possible. He wants to sabotage anything God plans to accomplish.

God's plan for restoring your personality has already taken into account the damage Satan has tried to inflict. His plan and His provision for setting you free are far more effective and powerful than your enemy's plan to keep you bound.

We are going to cover the subject of God's provision with a two-pronged approach. First, we will look at some of the kinds of hindrances referred to or implied in Hebrews 11. These were outlined in chapters 1 through 3. We'll compare the lie to the truth, and formulate some practical steps toward acting in the truth. Then in chapter 5 we will look at the way God has created the brain for storing memories. By His power He can detoxify those memories so that Satan's lies can longer do damage.

HINDERED BY SHAME

A sense of shame and unworthiness is a weight that can easily slow our forward motion. Committing sin automatically elicits shame. The first response to the first sin was shame—the feeling of being naked and exposed and needing to hide. Shame has been passed down through our spiritual genetic code.

Shame is an appropriate initial response to sin. Sin does expose who we are apart from Christ. Shame is beneficial when it shows us we cannot free ourselves from sin on our own. It forces us to realize we need the power of God through the indwelling life of Christ.

Even after we have accepted Christ and His full payment for our sins, when we commit sinful acts, or realize sinful attitudes we have been harboring, we feel ashamed. That appropriate shame is what leads us to repentance. We have come to view sin the same way God views it. Sin has become detestable to us, and we want to be free of it. When we sin, we can bring that sin immediately to the Father, who promises to forgive the sin because Jesus has already paid for it.

But let's look at inappropriate shame. Most of us, and I think all of us, have a generalized feeling of shame. We have the innate sense that if people could see us as we are, they would turn away. Most people have an occasionally recurring dream in which they are somehow publicly exposed—naked or inappropriately dressed for an occasion, or unprepared for a test. This sense of shame and fear of exposure is a universal human experience. It usually lies beneath the surface and is not necessarily identifiable, but it colors our lives and relationships.

That undercurrent of shame and sense of unworthiness works its way into our lives in ways too numerous to catalog. I think the enemy's most effective use of shame is to keep us from feeling welcomed into the Father's presence. It keeps us from ever feeling clean in His sight. We feel the need to rehearse again and again our failures and sins, begging His forgiveness and never really believing that He could completely forgive. We can't imagine that He could look at us and not see our many sins.

God knew that His forgiveness would be so foreign to us that He started laying the groundwork for our understanding early on. God built the concept into the daily experiences of His people by instituting the sacrificial system of worship. And even before the laws were given to Moses, God's people knew the necessity of blood sacrifice to atone for sins. We looked at the example of Abel, who knew that without the shedding of blood there is no covering of sin. But, conversely, once the blood had been offered, the sin was covered. God said so.

The ultimate reality to which the sacrificial system had always been pointing was Jesus. He shed His blood on the Cross as the once-for-all offering that would insure the forgiveness of our sins. Every sin. Past, present, future. Every single sin.

Let me point you to a poignant picture in God's sacrificial laws. A sinner brought a sin offering—a spotless animal. The priest examined the sin offering minutely to be sure it was the required offering, that it met all the standards. Once the priest had approved the offering, then the sinner could continue with the prescribed ritual. See this: the priest did not examine the sinner. He examined the sinner's sacrifice. Your sacrifice has been offered, and examined. The proclamation from heaven, spoken through Pilate's lips, was "I find no fault in Him." When we insist on nursing shame and embracing it, we are discounting the Sacrifice that God said cleared your record.

WHITE AS SNOW

What should we do when that feeling of shame overwhelms us, and we find no pleasure in the Lord's company because of it? Perhaps you have even found ways to avoid a sense of His presence. I invite you to use your visual imagination with me. Imagine your life written out. Imagine sheets and sheets of white paper covered in black print. Every single thought, every single action, every detail of your life recorded, nothing left out. Right there in black and white for anyone to see. Are you horrified?

Now look again. Huge portions of your life have been blotted out. Paragraphs and pages, covered over. But as you continue to look, you realize that those obscured portions are covered, not in black, but in red. Ah, covered by blood!

Then you say to yourself, "But what if someone could scrape off the covering? What if someone took a sharp instrument and uncovered all my sins? Then I'd be left exposed again. They're all just hidden and waiting to be uncovered."

Now you need to know a secret about blood. Blood not only covers; it absorbs. The blood in your body absorbs toxins and washes them away. It is a characteristic of blood, designed so by the Father for our understanding, that it absorbs. So, if someone could scrape off the blood covering all your sins, do you know what they would find? Snow white paper. Your sins, which were scarlet, have become as white as snow.

FEEL CLEAN

Have you confessed your sins? Then your faithful, just Father has forgiven them. He has washed them away. They have been absorbed into the blood of the Lamb. Fix your mind on that reality. Deliberately reject the lie. Allow yourself to feel clean.

It will take some time to reorient your mind, but you can do it, empowered by His Spirit. There is something effective about making declarative statements of the truth. Come up with a sentence that says what you need to believe, like "I'm clean." Every time the lie surfaces, say the truth. A thousand times a day if you need to. Say it out loud if you are alone, but say it.

Whatever it is that you avoid because of your sense of shame and unworthiness, do those things. Risk it. Deliberately go against what the lie tells you. Rebel.

Gradually the lie will recede and the truth will define your life. The many ways in which shame and a sense of worthlessness have affected your relationships, or your ability to risk, or your willingness to reach out will begin to self-correct. Under the Holy Spirit's tutelage, you will begin to recognize many behaviors and attitudes as rooted in shame, and you will change course and begin to prove the truth instead of feed the lie.

HINDERED BY LEGALISM

Let's move on to another hindrance: legalism. I realize that it is hard to define legalism. God does call us to obedience. He has established laws that are meant to protect us. We do need to exercise Spirit-enabled discipline to choose between right and wrong. But legalism is something different from being committed to obedience.

I think there are major differences between our love-motivated obedience and legalism. Remember Enoch, who walked with God. The Scripture's description of Enoch suggests that he became caught up in his personal walk with the Lord. That was where Enoch's attention was—the pleasure of His presence. One difference between legalism and obedience is the focus. If you notice that your walk of obedience is a burden, if it is draining you and causing you anxiety, or if you are often worried about whether you are breaking a rule, put it before the Lord for Him to help you see if legalism has slipped in.

Another difference between obedience and legalism is the effect each produces in our lives. If you are caught in legalism, you might find that your obedience to the laws of God gives you a sense of superiority. Do you find yourself looking down on others whom you perceive as less rule-following than you are? Or, does your focus on the rules give you a measuring stick against which to measure others, and decide who is and isn't measuring up? If your walk of obedience is leaving you with a judgmental and critical attitude, you are likely being hindered by legalism.

Yet another difference between obedience and legalism is that legalism will often put the most emphasis on outward behaviors and ignore inner attitudes. What did Jesus say to the world-class rule-followers, the religious elite of His day? "Woe to you, teachers of the law and Pharisees, you hypocrites! You are like whitewashed tombs, which look beautiful on the outside but on the inside are full of dead men's bones and everything unclean. In the same way, on the outside you appear to people as righteous but on the inside you are full of hypocrisy and wickedness" (Matthew 23:27–28).

We are not to ignore commands regarding behavior. There is a loving and productive and protective purpose for those commands. However, if we adhere to the outward forms of behavior and give no thought to the attitudes and positions of the heart, then we have missed the point altogether.

Recently I received an email from a woman who had been hurt and humiliated by someone she considered a mature Christian. This newly saved mother of a teenager was asked to bring some snack food for a youth party, and she brought some potato chips. In front of other parents, one of the pillars of the church made the comment, "I never buy that brand of chips. They are manufactured by [a beer company]." May I say for the record, I'm all for avoiding helping some industries prosper. Nevertheless, even if you can see the woman's thinking as legitimate, still was it more important than the tender heart of a baby in Christ? Here, I think, would be the difference between obedience and legalism. If the accuser had lived by the standard of her conscience, then that would be obedience. When she used her rule to devastate another, then that became legalism.

Another difference between obedience and legalism is that some people use legalistic, ultra-strict rule-following, even adding rules as they go, to compensate for the shame they themselves feel. Sometimes this shame is the wrongly placed sense of shame we just looked at. Sometimes it is shame over an inner compulsion that they struggle with. Instead of turning inward and allowing the deep healing of the Holy Spirit in that area, they turn the struggle outward and try to find more and more rules to follow and to impose on those around them. Each time they follow one of their rules, it temporarily relieves the guilt and shame of their inner struggle. If that description fits you, then right now you might feel shaken and exposed. You don't know what to do. Be assured, you are not alone. There is nothing for which the Lord does not have provision. Facing the reality is the first step to freedom.

How is legalism a hindrance and a weight to be thrown aside? Legalism keeps our eyes on ourselves instead of on Jesus. When the most zealous law-keepers of Jesus's day met Him, they were so blinded by their version of the law that they did not recognize the Living Law in front of them.

LAYING LEGALISM ASIDE

Did you recognize anything in these descriptions about yourself? I suspect that we all have at least a hint of legalism in us. Legalism fits our flesh nicely. Our flesh likes to have a measuring stick or a grading scale. It's far more comfortable. But what God calls us to is a step-by-step obedience. Not a rule-following obedience, but a Ruler-following obedience.

Notice how Jesus told us to obey Him: "If you obey my commands, you will remain in my love, just as I have obeyed my Father's commands and remain in his love" (John 15:10). He told us to obey Him the same way that He obeyed the Father. How did Jesus obey the Father? Moment by moment. Jesus walked so intimately with the Father that in any given situation, He could hear what the Father was saying.

Obedience goes beyond legalism. There was no rule for Jesus to follow that said, "Thou shalt feed 5,000 people with a loaf of bread and a few fishes." Obedience flows spontaneously from the one who has his ear pressed against the Father's heart to hear its every desire. To be satisfied with merely following rules is likely to cause us to miss out on fuller obedience.

We need to recognize and confess any legalism. Ask the Holy Spirit for discernment to recognize when you are responding in legalism instead of obedience. Get your heart and attention focused on the living Jesus indwelling you right now. Make Him the center of your thoughts day and night. At those moments when I am deliberately choosing obedience over sin,

I say something like this: "Only for You, only through You." It's just a little shorthand prayer that reminds me that my obedience is nothing of me and has no purpose to me except to let Jesus be Jesus through me. When you shed legalism to embrace loving obedience, you will walk in a new level of freedom. You will be free to serve others and care for them instead of competing and comparing.

Lay Aside the World's Influence

Remember that Noah was a righteous man living in the midst of a perverse generation. He was not infected by the sin and evil around him. Like Noah, we are called to live in the world, but not be of the world. Jesus prayed:

> *"My prayer is not that you take them out of the world but that you protect them from the evil one. They are not of the world, even as I am not of it. Sanctify them by the truth; your word is truth. As you sent me into the world, I have sent them into the world. For them I sanctify myself, that they too may be truly sanctified."*
> —John 17:15–19

God means for us to be in the world. We are to be the salt and the light. But we are not to absorb the world's values or behaviors. We are to be resistant to the influences of the world's system. James says that we are to "keep [ourselves] from being polluted by the world" (James 1:27).

When we looked earlier at Noah, who was unhindered in his walk by the surrounding evil, we saw that he was perhaps symbolized by the ark he was called to build. He was resistant to the sea of sin in which he lived, like the ark was resistant to the water by which it was surrounded. That's what Jesus prayed for us when He said, "Sanctify them by the truth." To sanctify means to set apart as holy—to remove from common use and designate for God's use. Something that is sanctified is kept separate. How does Jesus say we will be sanctified? By the truth. And what is truth? "Your word is truth."

Jesus has sent us into the world. That is our assignment. "As you sent me into the world, I have sent them into the world." He has made provision for us to be living in the world and yet be protected from its warping influence. What is that provision? He will sanctify you by His Word.

When we are continually filling our minds with His Word, the truth is building a barrier against the infiltration of the world. We are covering our lives with something in the spiritual realm that is represented by pitch in the material realm. Truth is a substance that coats, fills in the gaps, covers over, and makes us world-proof.

The one and only way that water could have gotten inside the ark was if someone opened the door before God gave the all clear. Do you remember the story of Noah, how patiently he had to wait before opening the ark's door? He had to be sure all the water was evaporated before he could risk opening the door. In spite of the careful construction and the barrier of pitch, the water could have rushed in through the open door.

Are there ways in which you open the door to the influences of the world? What are the world's influences? The world's values are the opposite of what God wants in your life. For example, God wants His people to live in unity. If you willingly listen to and engage in gossip about another believer, you are opening the door to the world's value: build yourself up by tearing someone else down. God wants His people to be honest and have complete integrity. If you find little ways to shade the truth or cut corners, then you are opening the door to the world's values. Certainly there are obvious ways to open the door through addictions and abuses, through filling your mind with ungodly images in media of all sorts. I don't have to list all the ways. You get the picture. We make choices that either keep the door shut to hindering influences or open it wide. When you find yourself opening the door, stop. Mentally close it. Lock it. Walk away.

Clothe yourselves with the Lord Jesus Christ, and do not think about how to gratify the desires of the sinful nature.
—Romans 13:14

Submit yourselves, then, to God. Resist the devil, and he will flee from you. Come near to God and he will come near to you.
—James 4:7–8

For the sake of our calling, we must keep the door closed to anything that would dilute our witness to the world around us. The passion to bring Christ to the world will compel us to pursue holiness.

Missionary Amy Carmichael wrote: "Anything that would hinder us from the closest walk that is possible to us till we see Him face to face, is not for us. We need to be sensitive to the first approach of the hindering thing. For the sake of the souls that may be stumbled if we turn even ever so little aside, for the sake of our Master's glory—dearer surely to us than all else—let us ask Him now to show us whether in anywise we have been showing 'crooked patterns.'"

So we know that we must resist the world's entangling influences. On the other end of the spectrum, we might become so afraid of being contaminated by the world that we run away and hide. This is not what Jesus called us to. He called us into the world. He called us to be His agents in the world. We can't do that in hiding. We can't engage our culture if we are hidden away. We can't influence those around us if they feel cut off from us. We can't be aware of needs if we keep ourselves isolated.

Do everything without complaining or arguing, so that you may become blameless and pure, children of God without fault in a crooked and depraved generation, in which you shine like stars in the universe as you hold out the word of life.
—Philippians 2:14–16

He has promised us that He has made provision to protect us in the world. His Word even goes so far as to say we will shine like stars. We can trust Him. Take advantage of His provision by marinating your life in His Word, by living a praying life, by being actively engaged with the body of Christ, by engaging in the spiritual disciplines.

As you take risks for God, His Spirit will be unleashed through you. Think about it: Do you have friends or family who need to know Christ? How many people in your neighborhood live apart from God's love? Who is hurting (spiritually, financially, relationally) in your community? at your office? How can you get to know and serve the needs of the poor and the lost near you or around the world?

You can fearlessly engage your culture and live unhindered, courageous in your calling. You can be out on the front lines of the battle because you are covered in God's armor. He hasn't sent you into battle unsupplied.

Discussion

1. Why does God convict us of sin?

2. Sin steals our _____.

3. Do you agree that everything that hinders us has sin at its root? Why or why not?

4. How is unhealthy shame a hindrance?

5. What are the differences between legalism and obedience? How does legalism hinder?

6. Review the concepts and identify insights that relate to some or all of the four characteristics of fully free people.

   - Be vehicles through which God's Spirit will be unleashed in the world.

   - Be leaders of influence and uncompromised integrity.

   - Be courageous in their calling and engaged in their culture.

   - Be passionate about God as they step out and take risks together with other believers.

CHAPTER 5

Detaching

Some hindrances, like those we explored in the previous chapter, seem to be part of our personalities. Except for the Holy Spirit's precision surgery—separating out the patterns of our flesh from the ways the Spirit is leading us—those hindrances would live undetected in us. Have you watched a movie or television show in which a crime scene investigator looks at a setting and sees no apparent sign of blood, but then he sprays his luminol, and under fluorescent light, the blood is revealed. That is kind of like what the Holy Spirit is doing in us. His presence reveals hindrances that are so enmeshed in our nature that they do not appear on the surface to be sins. They seem to be just a natural part of our personalities and only the light of His presence exposes the truth. "In your light we see light" (Psalm 36:9). As He reveals hindrances and begins to clear our lives of them, we then experience a freedom we never dreamed possible.

In the progressive discovery of freedom, we realize time and again what freedom looks like. As hindrances are exposed and then thrown aside, freedom leads us into unfettered, all-in, no-holds-barred ministry. Risk-taking courage is our new normal. This new freedom is addictive, intoxicating. The more you experience, the more you crave. You were born for this!

So, the freedom march continues. We realize that while some hindrances are carried around inside us as part of our personalities, other hindrances are things, persons, relationships, or events outside us that keep us bound to them, drawing us back into Egypt-like bondage.

LAY ASIDE OUR ATTACHMENTS

Remember Abraham's initial call. "Abraham, you go out to a place I'll show you." God called Abraham to leave the familiar and the comfortable and set out for "a land I'll show you."

Without anything tangible in hand, Abraham had to let go of everything he could see and embrace what he couldn't see. Like Abraham, God is calling us to let go of people, places, and things. Even when they are in our possession, we do not own them. Everything we have is God's, entrusted to our care for a time. The danger is that we let these things wrap themselves around us and we come to think of them as ours by right. When we learn to be *altared* in all areas of our lives, then we can run the race unhindered by attachments.

Paul describes how to live the *altared* life: "May I never boast except in the cross of our Lord Jesus Christ, through which the world has been crucified to me, and I to the world" (Galatians 6:14). The only thing that belongs to us and to which we can cling is the Cross of our Lord Jesus Christ. In order to cling to the power of that Cross, we have to let go of everything else.

Be ready to go when God says go. Be ready to let go of what you can see and embrace what you can't see. As He proved with Abraham, He is never calling you to relinquish just for the sake of sacrificing, but so that He can fill your hand with something new. Something you've never seen before. Something He will cause you to see.

Moses's challenge was similar. If he was going to fulfill the call for which he was born, he would have to let go of everything he knew to embrace what he didn't know. He had to decide what he valued. What owned his heart? The security and comfort of Egypt, or the call of God? He had to live in an *altared* state. A living offering. God spent 40 years extracting Egypt from Moses's heart so that he could return and not be possessed by its attractions. He could go back to Egypt with only one goal—to lead his people out.

Here's what I do occasionally to remind myself that I am living in an *altared* state. I walk through my house and office and surrender everything. Things in my house and office represent other things that need to be surrendered. Pictures of my children. The books I've authored. The ministry I'm involved in. My checkbook. My past. I have a little ceremony — just me and God. I build an altar in my heart and let go of anything that I might hesitate to leave behind when the Lord says to go.

HINDERED BY A MISPLACED FOCUS

You might be hindered by focusing on your circumstances. Your situation might be distracting you from seeing where the real action is.

When we keep our attention on the need instead of the supply, we are consumed with that need. It seems to grow bigger, and time seems to slow down. If instead we reframe the situation and begin to see it in terms of God's provision — making Him the focal point — then the situation looks different.

When you walk in faith, you will train your eyes to see the reality of the spiritual realm rather than the facts as your senses perceive them. With practice, this will become your natural way of seeing things. My friend Joanne, whose daughter is a photographer, had this thought. Remember the days when we shot photographs on film and developed them from a negative? Have you ever looked at the negative of a photograph? It is exactly the opposite of the photograph. Where the photograph is light, the negative is dark. Where the photograph is dark, the negative is light. Hold the negative up to the light and the scene changes. What appeared to be dark is really light. The true picture emerges. Let Him show you that every negative, when held up to the Light, becomes a positive. Practice until your automatic response to any fearful, critical, negative thought is faith. *Learn* to see the positive. It will make all the difference.

Keeping your focus on God takes discipline and decisiveness. You have to stick with it until this way of thinking becomes your normal reaction. Like every learned behavior, what starts with conscious effort and determination, evolves into something that comes naturally. Effort — empowered by the Holy

Spirit—leads to effortlessness, or what the writer of Hebrews calls "rest." He says: "Let us, therefore, *make every effort* to enter that rest" (Hebrews 4:11, emphasis mine). There is a walk of discipline and integrity that leads to rest. It starts with choosing to cooperate with the Spirit and deliberately relinquishing your own best ideas and efforts to His indwelling power. Little by little, you give control to the Spirit as if on autopilot.

The famous eighteenth-century American pastor Jonathan Edwards compiled a list of resolutions that spelled out how he would live with eternity in focus rather than be tossed about by life's changing circumstances. Let me commend a few to you.

Resolved, that I will do whatsoever I think to be most to God's glory....

Resolved to do whatever I think to be my duty and most for the good and advantage of mankind in general. Resolved to do this, whatever difficulties I meet with, how many soever, and how great soever.

Resolved, never to lose one moment of time; but improve it the most profitable way I possibly can.

Resolved, to live with all my might, while I do live. Resolved, never to do anything, which I should be afraid to do, if it were the last hour of my life.

Resolved, never to do any thing out of revenge.

Resolved, never to speak evil of anyone...upon no account except for some real good.

Resolved, to do always, what I can towards making, maintaining, and preserving peace....

Resolved, not only to refrain from an air of dislike, fretfulness, and anger in conversation, but to exhibit an air of love, cheerfulness and benignity.

Consider making a list of your own resolutions by which you can discipline your thoughts and attitudes until the new ways become your norm. Here are some suggestions to reorient your focus toward God and others:

Let anxiety and worry be a trigger to turn to praise. Praise is what brings God and His greatness to center stage in our minds. When worry starts whispering, begin to praise God. Make praise your habit all the time.

Become involved with a small prayer group. In a small group, other people's situations become as important to you as your own, and you are not consumed with your circumstances. Also, as you build up a history with a prayer group, you can observe how God is working at different stages in different situations. For example, someone in the group has an ongoing prayer need, but you have seen progress. You can say, "Remember how things were a year ago when we started praying for this. Remember that it looked completely out of control and hopeless. And look at it now—how far things have come." Then you can say to yourself, "One year from now, I'll be saying the same thing about my situation." When we are consumed by the present, with no perspective, it's harder to keep our focus on God's power. Finally, a small prayer group will help bear your burden. They'll be there to cheer you on and encourage you and help you refocus.

Don't give voice to fear. I don't mean don't talk about your troubling circumstances. But I am saying skip the fearful commentary: "Things will never change. It's too late now. Things only go from bad to worse." When you say such things, it just reinforces fear in your mind. You are lining up with the lie. Instead, say the truth, even when you don't feel like you believe it at the moment. "God is in control. God is working out everything toward His good resolution. God loves and cherishes me."

You'll find your own ways to be disciplined about keeping your focus right. Just do it. Don't allow your circumstances to distract you from the provision God has put in place. Shift your focus from yourself to God. And then follow His lead into service to the world.

Hindered by Misplaced Attachments to Those We Love

The call for Abraham to offer his son, his only son, as an offering was not so that Isaac would die, but so that Abraham would die. The Abraham who wanted to possess and manage and own — that Abraham had to die. A new Abraham had to be created on his heart's altar. What would be harder than laying yourself on the altar? Laying your son on the altar. That cuts deep.

Just like God gave Isaac to Abraham, God has given the people you love to you. He is not saying not to love them and nurture them and pour yourself out for them. He is saying don't own them, and don't let them own you.

There comes a time in every relationship when you have to let go of the one you love. You have to stop fixing and managing and meddling and manipulating. You have to let go. This is part of the call to love them. You have to step out of the way and let God do everything He wants to do in their lives, and everything He wants to do in yours.

When I pray for my children, I say it this way — to remind myself: "Lord, here's Your Brantley." Then I go on to pray over him. And on to the next one, and the next one. Through the day, as my children come to mind, I see their faces in my mind and I just say, "Yours." Shorthand prayer.

When the times come — as they always do — when those I love dearly have difficulties I wish I could solve for them, I come more quickly to the place of surrender, because I try to stay there all the time. It is still a struggle and I have to make sure I am bound to the altar, but I am working on making it my first inclination rather than my last resort.

You may not have biological children, but you have spiritual children, and you have people you love and whom you tend to feel possessive of and protective of. *Altared* living means that you are not hindering your own walk, or the walks of those you love, by possessive love.

Missionary Jim Elliot wrote the following words to his parents: "I do not wonder that you are saddened at the word of my going to South America. . . . Grieve not, then, if your sons seems to desert you, but rejoice, rather, seeing the will of God done gladly. Remember how the Psalmist described children? He said that they were as an heritage from the Lord, and that every man should be happy who had his quiver full of them. And what is a quiver full of but arrows? And what are arrows for but to shoot? So with the strong arm of prayer, draw the bowstring back and let the arrows fly—all of them straight at the Enemy's hosts."

HINDERED BY TIES TO THE PAST

When the children of Israel left Egypt behind it was to be a complete break. They could not be hindered in their forward motion by ties to the old life. When they crossed the Red Sea, Paul calls it a baptism.

> *For I do not want you to be ignorant of the fact, brothers, that our forefathers were all under the cloud and that they all passed through the sea. They were all baptized into Moses in the cloud and in the sea.*
> —1 Corinthians 10:1–3

What does Paul have in mind when he refers to it as baptism? It was a death to the old life and a resurrection to the new. This new life was so completely new that they started a new calendar, one that marked the journey toward the Red Sea as the first month. "The LORD said to Moses and Aaron in Egypt, 'This month is to be for you the first month, the first month of your year'" (Exodus 12:1–2).

God had to do deep work in them to bring them into the promise. They spent years in the wilderness, looking back. They couldn't fully experience their freedom because they still thought like slaves. They had too many memories and emotional ties to their past.

What keeps you tied to your past? One of the strongest ties that keep us looking back is unforgiveness. Unforgiveness keeps us connected to our offender and gives that offender power over us. It even extends the offender's reach, allowing that offense to impact those we love and influence. The writer of Hebrews warns us: "See to it that no one misses the grace of

God and that no bitter root grows up to cause trouble and defile many" (Hebrews 12:15–16). A root of bitterness in your life can reach into the lives of everyone around you. That root may be firmly fixed in your past, but is now destroying your present.

Even the most grievous sins against us need to be forgiven. This is not for the sake of the offender, but for our sakes. We are not meant to carry bitterness. It holds us back and slows us down. It gives our enemy an opening: "And what I have forgiven—if there was anything to forgive—I have forgiven in the sight of Christ for your sake, in order that Satan might not outwit us. For we are not unaware of his schemes" (2 Corinthians 2:10–11).

Let me share something from my book *He Leads Me Beside Still Waters*:

> I have found Jesus' words, "they do not know what they are doing," to be extremely important in learning to forgive. I believe this is nearly always true. The one who offended you does not really know what he or she is doing. A large percentage of the offenses against us are entirely unintentional. Most of the time, your offender has no idea how you have perceived his actions or words.
>
> Even when a person's words or actions are deliberately unkind or harsh, as were the soldiers' who were crucifying Jesus, the person does not fully understand the ramifications. Strange as it seems, even a person who appears to be intentionally harming you has been blinded by the enemy to the whole picture. Your enemy is not flesh and blood. The human heart is deceitful—able to fool itself. Forgive him. Forgive her. Let it go. They do not know what they are doing.

Let the forgiving process begin. Work it through all the way. You will know you have forgiven when you can remember the incident without the anger, and when your anger toward your offender can become compassion. You will be free of that tie that keeps pulling you back into your past.

Another way that we can be tangled up by our past is through memories of events that have scarred us and have allowed certain lies to take root. These memories are often not part of our conscious thought processes, but still are creating chaos in our present situations. God has provision for healing us of the soul wounds that have become infected and are spreading their infection throughout our personalities.

Author Becky Harling tells her brave story of forgiving her abuser in her book *Rewriting Your Emotional Script*:

I lay facedown on my bedroom floor and told the Lord that I wanted to forgive but that I didn't know how. I began to pray, *Holy Spirit, I am petrified of revisiting those horrible moments, but if You will lead me, I will follow You even there.*

The Holy Spirit was more than willing. It was as if He led me down a long, dark corridor, opening door after door. Behind each door I saw a little girl being sexually abused. She tried to scream for help, but no words came out of her mouth.

Each time I watched another episode of abuse, the Holy Spirit whispered, "Becky, will you dare to give me your hurt? Your pain? Your anger and your fear? Will you forgive?"

Between broken sobs, I whispered, "yes." When I finished four hours later, I felt exhausted but also free from fear and anger.

That day was the beginning of my journey to forgive the one who had abused me. Yes, it was only the beginning. For years I had resisted forgiving the person who had done such evil toward me, yet I knew that if I wanted to move ahead emotionally and spiritually, I had to take this step. Forgiving my abuser has not been simple, nor easy. Indeed, it has been gut-wrenching. Sometimes I feel I have completed the journey and then the Holy Spirit reveals another layer of anger or resentment tied to the abuse. Once again, I must affirm my decision to forgive.

Like Becky, you will experience freedom through forgiving. You will break the power of anger and hurt as you do the most unnatural thing imaginable: forgive as God, in Christ, forgave you (see Ephesians 4:32).

HINDERED BY HARDENED OPINIONS

As with the Israelites at Jericho, God will sometimes call us to unorthodox and creative methods. Not new doctrine, just new ways. If we have clamped the door down on new ideas, we are likely to miss the most exciting parts of God's call in our lives.

One way we can be hindered from answering God's call is by being resistant to new avenues of service. If you find yourself saying, "Oh, no. That's not my strength," consider that God may be about to show you a new strength. It takes the Spirit to discern here, because we are all asked to do things that are not in line with our calling and we have to learn where and when to say no. But be sure that you don't have an automatic response that shuts the door on new directions. Give God free rein to stretch you and lead you to step out and take risks.

A resistance to new ways might also come out in your reaction to others. "That's not how it's done!" or "That's never going to work!" or "We've never done it that way before!" I think Satan's favorite might be: "We tried that once." Again, it takes the Spirit's real-time guidance. We are certainly not called to discount the wisdom gained through experience, but we don't have to be tied to the past.

We all have strong opinions, even hardened opinions, about issues, and I think we all assume that our opinions are right and righteous. Here is the challenge: Set your opinion aside. Listen, explore, pray, be willing. Ask for clear guidance and be opinionless until God shows you. Be open to His new directions. Humble yourself and be willing to have one of your favorite opinions shattered. Even if it turns out that your original thought was correct, I imagine that there will at least be some correction to it.

How do you respond to other believers who—how shall I say this?—have a different fashion sense than yours? Do you have a list of rules for how others are supposed to dress for church? Or how they are supposed to adorn themselves, or not adorn themselves? Do you automatically turn away from someone with a piercing you don't like? Or a tattoo that doesn't appeal to you? Do you mentally chalk them up as less spiritual than you are? Is it possible that your rules in this area just don't apply?

Don't be hindered in your journey by being unwilling to listen to new ideas. God is always an innovator. Every new idea or new way of doing eternal work has an eternal underpinning. God isn't making up new ideas really, just new ways to express eternal, never-changing ideas. What may seem to be a risk to us isn't really much of a risk when God is behind it.

Missionary Hudson Taylor, who pioneered missions work in China and established the China Inland Mission, did so in unorthodox ways for which he endured much criticism. He especially invited controversy when he began to dress in the style of the Chinese to whom he was called. He wore their clothing and wore his hair in their style, lived among them in a hut like theirs, ate their food. Over and over he heard, "This not how we do it! This has never been done before!" But Taylor held firm to his calling and risked the approval of his peers to follow the call that defined his life. Taylor went beyond what was accepted and endured the scorn of those who clung to tradition, but in so doing, he saw the fulfillment of the vision God had given him as a penniless teenager. Years of dedicated missionary service, filled with disappointments and sorrows, birthed a spiritual movement that is still impacting the whole of China today.

LAY ASIDE EVERY HINDRANCE

Satan wants to exploit these hindrances to slow us down. But we don't have to get stuck. God commands us to lay these weights aside. Throw them off. Strip down for the race. If He commands it, then He provides it. Be intentional in recognizing those things that might slow your stride. Then be intentional about letting God show you His provision for how to toss them aside and pick up the pace. God wants you to be free for Him to use. You can live life unhindered.

Discussion

1. Do you recognize attachments that keep holding you back?

2. What relationships do you need to surrender?

3. What unforgiveness and hurtful memories are hindering your progress?

4. Are there any places where your focus needs to be realigned?

5. Review the concepts and identify insights that relate to some or all of the four characteristics of fully free people.

   - Be vehicles through which God's Spirit will be unleashed in the world.

   - Be leaders of influence and uncompromised integrity.

   - Be courageous in their calling and engaged in their culture.

   - Be passionate about God as they step out and take risks together with other believers.

CHAPTER 6

Hardwired for Healing

To recap: God has commanded us to lay aside the hindering weight of the sin that so easily wraps itself around us and trips us up. He never commands what He does not provide. Our challenge is to be alert for the provision and cooperate with Him in putting His provision to work.

Years ago, as a college student first ardently seeking the fullness of God's presence, I was moved by an essay called "Holy Obedience" by Thomas R. Kelley, a Quaker educator. I didn't want religion, I wanted Him, and this essay spoke to me of the awesome possibility of having God's presence be my constant, immediate reality. Let me share a few words from Kelley as he reflects on the inner drama of every believer who seeks to fully obey.

It is the drama of the Hound of Heaven baying relentlessly upon the track of man. It is the drama of the lost sheep wandering in the wilderness, restless and lonely, feebly searching, while over the hills comes the wiser Shepherd. For His is a shepherd's heart, and restless until He holds His sheep in His arms. It is the drama of the Eternal Father drawing the prodigal home unto Himself, where there is bread enough and to spare.... And always its chief actor is—the Eternal God of Love.

God the initiator, God the aggressor, God the seeker, God the stirrer into life, God the ground of our obedience, God the giver of the power to become children of God.

As we continue to consider our obedience in light of God's promises revealed through His commands, keep in mind that He is all. He doesn't call us to obey, and then step out of the picture, hoping we make it. He is there from first to last, providing Himself. He has already worked into the DNA of creation the mechanisms by which we can leave our past behind and throw off the chains of damaging memories.

The Scripture tell us, "For by him all things were created: things in heaven and on earth, visible and invisible, whether thrones or powers or rulers or authorities; all things were created by him and for him" (Colossians 1:16). Nothing exists that He did not create. Every detail of everything owes its existence to Him. "All things were created *by* him and *for* him" (emphasis mine). In other words, when He created all things, He created them for His own use. He designed everything He created so that it serves His purposes. Every created thing is arranged so that it accomplishes His plan. He has provided for us to be able to throw off every hindrance, and that provision is incorporated into His blueprint for creation.

He designed human beings to have a will that operates freely. The entrance of sin disrupted that design, and sin, as always, works contrary to God's plan. Paul says of anyone who would be the Lord's servant: "Those who oppose him he must gently instruct, in the hope that God will grant them repentance leading them to a knowledge of the truth, and that they will come to their senses and escape from the trap of the devil, *who has taken them captive to do his will*" (2 Timothy 2:25–26, emphasis mine). Sin, first entered into freely, soon becomes a tyrannical captor. Again, Paul describes this condition.

We know that the law is spiritual; but I am unspiritual, sold as a slave to sin. I do not understand what I do. For what I want to do I do not do, but what I hate I do. And if I do what I do not want to do,

I agree that the law is good. As it is, it is no longer I myself who do it, but it is sin living in me.
—Romans 7:14–17

A person apart from Christ is described as a captive and a slave. Jesus came to set captives free. When He saved you, He set your will free to function as it was meant to function. Aligned with Christ, we have the ability to choose freely. By choosing Him and His way over and over again, we can use our God-designed and God-empowered free will to shake off the last vestiges of our old ways. We can be rebuilt and restored to our original design.

Look at the following promise. Put your name in place of "Judah and Israel" and "this city."

> *"I will bring health and healing to it; I will heal my people and will let them enjoy abundant peace and security. I will bring Judah and Israel back from captivity and will rebuild them as they were before. I will cleanse them from all the sin they have committed against me and will forgive all their sins of rebellion against me. Then this city will bring me renown, joy, praise and honor before all nations on earth that hear of all the good things I do for it; and they will be in awe and will tremble at the abundant prosperity and peace I provide for it."*
> —Jeremiah 33:6–9

God plans for your healing, wholeness, and restoration. He has it in mind. He is working toward it day and night. Whether you are awake or asleep, God is moving you in the direction of healing and freedom. He has made you heal-able. (Yes, I made up another word.)

SOUL SALVE

We are all riddled with soul wounds and, if left to fester, their noxious effect oozes into our personalities, our relationships, and our emotions, and poisons our thought patterns. Open those wounds to the healing balm of the Spirit of God, allowing the Healer Himself to detoxify your soul. He can speak His Word into the recesses of your heart, rooting out lies and replacing them with truth.

"May God himself, the God of peace, sanctify [detoxify, cleanse] you through and through. May your whole spirit, soul and body be kept [guarded from loss or injury] blameless [healthy, without weakness] at the coming of our Lord Jesus Christ. The one who calls you is faithful and he will do it" (1 Thessalonians 5:23–24, words in brackets added).

The soul could be defined as your personality or your human nature. Many theologians describe the soul as including your mind, your will, and your emotions—all the parts of you that Jesus wants to restore and heal and free. Christ in you expresses Himself through your personality.

The memories that keep you tied to your past, hindering you and entangling you, are in your mind. As you set out now to experience His healing and His wholeness, get this fixed in your mind: your healing is within you. He is your healing, and He is in you. Healing does not come as some by-product of your faith, but instead comes directly from the indwelling Jesus, whom F. B. Meyer describes as the living Fountain rising up in the well of our personality.

You are surrendering yourself in deeper and more meaningful ways to His lordship. Opening your life to His presence is opening your life to His healing. His healing does not come separately from Himself. His healing presence begins to permeate your mind, your will, and your emotions, infusing your personality with His power—a process similar to the yeast that leavens the whole loaf. Healing spreads to your mind, your memories, your instinctive responses, your emotions, your perceptions.

"Above all else, guard your heart, for it is the wellspring of life" (Proverbs 4:23). The Hebrew word translated "heart" could accurately be translated "mind." It is the center of thought, reasoning, and emotion. Your mind is the wellspring of life. A wellspring is the source from which the river flows. All of your reactions, responses, and emotions flow from your mind. If the source, the wellspring, is contaminated, then what flows from it will be too. "The good man brings good things out of the good stored up in him, and the evil man brings evil things out of the evil stored up in him" (Matthew 12:35).

God is at work in you in the deep places. He is healing wounded areas of your personality. Soul salve is being applied in your life right now. We need to learn to participate in the healing, increasing its effectiveness. As we cooperate with Jesus, we are throwing off hindrances.

BRAIN WASHING

Jesus said that we are made clean by the Word. "You are already clean because of the word I have spoken to you" (John 15:3). Speaking of the church, He said that He would "make her holy, cleansing her by the washing with water through the word" (Ephesians 5:26–27). He prayed, "Sanctify them by the truth. Your word is truth" (John 17:17).

The first way that Jesus begins to clean us out inside is by speaking His Word in His present-tense, living voice. When you read the Scripture, when you meditate on the Scripture, and memorize the Scripture, hear His voice speaking to you. It washes your brain clean.

Soaking in the Scripture lets its living power penetrate into the marrow of your personality, changing every part of you. As the Word pours into you, the truth confronts lies you didn't even know you believed. It takes lies head-on and over-powers them.

Do you remember the very first video games? There was one called Pac-Man. I can't remember what the object of the game was, but I remember a big round head with a mouth over-took little dots and swallowed them up. That's all I remember. Chomp, chomp, chomp. Little dots disappearing into the giant head never to be seen again. That's my picture of how the living Word works on the inside. It overtakes and chomps down lies. Eats them alive.

The same voice that created the universe in the beginning is speaking to you now. The same Spirit who hovered over the chaos in the beginning and called order into being is living in you now. "By the word of the LORD were the heavens made, their starry host by the breath of his mouth" (Psalm 33:6). He still does His work by His Word.

Take the Word in and let it do its work. Expose yourself to all the Word of God you can, and trust that He will make it effective in your life. Read His Word. Meditate on His Word. Memorize His Word. Pray His Word. Sing His Word.

His Word is like water, He says. It washes clean. Think about water as it flows forcefully. It pushes obstacles out of its way. It dissolves dirt and grime—picks it up and carries it away. It reshapes the landscape. It splashes and sprays as it goes. Nothing is left the same in the wake of rushing waters. Nothing can stop its momentum. Flood your life with His Word.

MIND CONTROL

Many of our responses to the present are really coming from our past. We feel like we are responding to the present, but really we are responding out of our past experiences.

Beginning even in the womb, where a fetus can record sounds and emotions in memory, we construct a paradigm of reality that consists of stored memories. Most of those memories are not consciously recalled. In fact, many of those memories are stored only as impressions and emotions. Every experience we have in the present is filtered through a perception of reality that our minds have assembled over our lifetimes.

It is believed that the strongest controllers of personality and future responses are formulated in the first several years of life. A young child does not have context for evaluating situations. He stores them in his memory as they seem to him at the moment. For example, a child can't correctly evaluate an adult's anger, and so can only interpret it as "I'm bad." That will be how that memory is labeled in the mental filing system. When another incident occurs, then that memory will be filed and labeled and linked to other files. Throughout the years, when something happens that opens one memory file, all the files linked to it open as well. A small, innocuous experience will evoke an out-of-proportion response that seems to the person as if it is exactly proportional.

Our brains are created to store information in separate specialized areas. The part of your brain that stores factual memory—memory of events—is called the hippocampus. The part of your brain that stores emotional memory—the stored emotion from an event—is called the amygdala. The hippocampus is not fully developed before the age of three, but the amygdala is present from the time you are a fetus.

Therefore, early in life your brain may store an emotional memory without any factual memory to go with it. Only the emotion lives in your mind. This leaves us with emotions that need someplace to land. So, for instance, a person could repeatedly experience a generalized sense of fear in many current situations, triggered not by present reality but by an early childhood memory. The person could be described as having a fearful personality. When asked why they're often afraid they might respond, "I don't know—that's how I've always been."

My friend Karen is on a healing journey. She recognizes that she has a lifelong pattern of being hurt and walking away. She gets hurt easily because she interprets many exchanges as rejection or criticism, even though she now realizes they were not meant that way. Her response has always been to leave the relationship behind.

As God is healing her, she explained to me recently, "It's not that I don't want to see that person again, but that I think that person doesn't want to see me again." When Karen's mother got mad at her as a child, she didn't want to see Karen. This response became the basis for a lie Karen believed that she must now reject. She still feels the same, but she is not responding in the same way to the lie. She is pushing past what her wounded personality tells her, responding in truth, and refusing to give up on relationships. The time will come when the truth will feel true to her.

DETOXIFYING MEMORIES

As you grow, your brain begins to store hurtful or fearful or joyful events as episodic memories. You store the whole episode, not just a fact or two. The more emotion that is attached to an event, the more memory cues we will associate with it. When an episode occurs that causes great anger, hurt, or resentment in you, your brain will store it as episodic memory. And episodic memory means that in storing the event, you have memorized many physical details. You can recall the room, the arrangement of the furniture, the stance and tone and facial expression of the other person, sounds and smells that were present, and other physical aspects. You can recreate the scene in your mind with much detail. Because of this, you often stumble across triggers that bring that memory out of storage.

For example, an episodic memory might have a certain smell associated with it. When you smell that aroma, it triggers the memory. The memory makes the past present. So, at a moment's notice, a memory with strong emotional content can rush at you and the anger or hurt can be as sharp as it was when the event first occurred.

In any memory, the emotional memory comes first, then the factual memory follows. Most people have developed good reflexes for pushing factual memory down quickly, but the emotion it engaged cannot be so easily dismissed. The emotion sits just under the surface and will have to be expressed somewhere. It may be turned outward or it may be turned inward. Are you beginning to see how some memories keep you tied to your past and can be a weight that holds you back?

Yet, instead of being stuck with the effects of those memories, God has made us healable. The very way our brains are structured leaves an opening for God to heal. He will not change the facts of the past, but He can cleanse the emotions tied to it.

God has made our brains so that emotion associated with an event is stored separately from the facts of the event. Researchers are doing promising experiments on post-traumatic stress disorder (PTSD) sufferers. These are people for whom a triggered memory is a traumatic event, and the memory makes the present unbearable. In one example, a woman traumatized by a rape was given blood pressure lowering medicines, then asked to remember the event. She was able to start remembering the event without the high emotion. As she deliberately re-experienced the event without the attached emotions, she began for the first time to make progress recovering from her PTSD.

I believe that God made our brains that way so He could use His own creation's design to heal. As He dwells in us, He can reach into those memories, even those of which we are not aware, and bring healing. You can invite Him into your emotional memory to do a deep work that He alone can do. He can remove the toxins from those memories and leave them powerless. While you can't erase what happened to you, God can heal the emotions tied to it. And this healing will affect everything associated with the memory.

You don't have to even consciously remember an event to ask the Spirit, who searches the deep and hidden things, to heal. "He reveals deep and hidden things; he knows what lies in darkness, and light dwells with him. I thank and praise you, O God of my fathers: You have given me wisdom and power, you have made known to me what we asked of you" (Daniel 2:22–23).

Living with other people affords many opportunities for being hurt or angered or disappointed. Your memory bank is filled with such events. But another thing to understand about episodic memory is that you will remember it as it seemed to you. It is a subjective memory. For example, a person might remember his childhood home as very large, only to visit it as an adult and discover it is really quite small. You have hurtful memories stored *from your viewpoint*. Many people have found that as they allow those memories to surface freely and look at them from an adult perspective, they can get a very different viewpoint. You will be able to forgive your offenders and let the emotion of the memory go.

This is far from a thorough treatment of the subject of toxic memories. But it will get you started. You can take control of the emotions you express before you express them. You can realize that what seems to be a proportional response to you in the moment is colored by past experiences and their emotions. You can start asking the indwelling Christ to root out the lie embedded in your remembered experience and plant truth in its place. You don't have to work hard or search for these memories. Just let the Healer do the healing work.

THROW OFF EVERY HINDRANCE

Author Thelma Wells experienced a childhood that might have left anyone bitter and angry. Thelma's mother was a severely deformed teenager with no husband and no place to go, since her abusive mother insisted that she take the baby and leave the house. So when Thelma was born, her unwed teenage mother found work as a maid cleaning "the big house" while living with her baby daughter in servants' quarters.

Eventually, the baby went to live with her great-grandparents, who called her Thelma Louise Smith and loved her dearly. They took little Thelma to church, where she learned to love the hymns and praise songs. On those occasions when Thelma was taken to her grandparents' home, her grandmother abused her, just as she had tormented Thelma's mother. She was locked in a dark, smelly, insect-infested closet until just before her grandfather came home. At that time her grandmother would bring her out of the closet, clean her up, and act as if all was well. In spite of her deep fear, little Thelma spent her time in the closet singing every hymn and praise song she could remember. She would sing herself to sleep in that closet, and the Lord received this little girl's innocent praise and rewarded it with an abundant life of joy, protecting her from feelings of anger or bitterness.

Thelma grew up to become a courageous trailblazer for black women, a prominent international speaker, consultant, and author, and a wife, mother, grandmother, and great-grandmother. She spends every day of her life encouraging others and facilitating freedom through her vibrant ministry.

Do you see how God used His own ingenious design to let little Thelma have an experience but attach different emotions to it? Her praises overrode and overcame her terror, leaving her with a positive emotional memory in spite of the terrible situation. We're designed that way. Right now, you can accept the facts of experiences that have hurt you, but reassign new emotions to them. Because you are fearfully and wonderfully made.

Decide now that you are not willing to be held back by any hindrance. Lay aside anything that weighs you down or slows your pace. Open your mind to the healing power of the Holy Spirit. His indwelling presence is always doing a deep healing work. He will not change the past, but He will detoxify the memories. Don't hold tightly to your memories. Let the Healer heal your past.

Discussion

1. Describe how sin becomes a tyrannical captor in our lives.

2. Do you recognize some ways that your memories might be holding you captive to sinful responses and reactions?

3. How has God hardwired us for healing?

4. Review the concepts and identify insights that relate to some or all of the four characteristics of fully free people.

    • Be vehicles through which God's Spirit will be unleashed in the world.

    • Be leaders of influence and uncompromised integrity.

    • Be courageous in their calling and engaged in their culture.

    • Be passionate about God as they step out and take risks together with other believers.

And let us run with perseverance the race marked out for us.

Key 3
His Power

CHAPTER 7

His Power in You

*W*e have looked at examples of people whose lives bore witness to God's faithfulness and served as the platform for His power. We have considered how to lay aside every hindrance to our own journey, making our lives available to be vehicles for His power. Now we will examine the next phrase in Hebrews 12:1, which introduces the race metaphor. By calling us to a race, He is also guaranteeing the power to run that race victoriously.

"Let us run with perseverance the race marked out for us" (Hebrews 12:1).

Why a race? After all, we're not in competition with one another. We're not trying to outdo each other. What is he communicating by calling our journey a race?

It seems that he is referring to a long-distance race. This race will take perseverance. In a long-distance race, the winner is not the fastest, nor the strongest, but the one with the most endurance. That's the secret of a long-distance runner: stamina.

This is a race "marked out for us" or "set before us." It has a definite course. It is a well-worn path. We have already seen that many have run the course ahead of us. We can use their footprints as something of a guide. The writer of Hebrews twice suggests this:

We want each of you to show this same diligence to the very end, in order to make your hope sure. We do not want you to become lazy, but to imitate those who through faith and patience inherit what has been promised.
—Hebrews 6:11–12

Consider the outcome of their way of life and imitate their faith.
—Hebrews 13:7–8

In every case we have been told to consider, one thing is consistent. Our race is a long-distance run. There is no quick-fix, microwaveable version. Faith, patience, endurance, and stamina are required. The kind of power that enables perseverance is exactly the kind of power Jesus has available.

How does He develop stamina in us?

We also rejoice in our sufferings, because we know that suffering produces perseverance; perseverance, character; and character, hope. And hope does not disappoint us, because God has poured out his love into our hearts by the Holy Spirit, whom he has given us.
—Romans 5:3–5

Consider it pure joy, my brothers, whenever you face trials of many kinds, because you know that the testing of your faith develops perseverance. Perseverance must finish its work so that you may be mature and complete, not lacking anything.
—James 1:4–5

Do you see the thread? We should welcome trials and suffering because through difficulties we experience, we will develop perseverance. It seems there is no other way to gain stamina but to have to put it to use. Notice another parallel thought in these two texts. Perseverance brings something valuable and solid into our lives. It's not just perseverance for the sake of perseverance, but perseverance as the doorway to something more.

Runners claim something called a "runner's high"—a euphoria that comes at a certain point in a long-distance run. But to get to the runner's high, they have to first break through what they call "the wall." At one point in the run, the runner experiences a strong desire to quit, like he can't go on. But if he doesn't give up when he feels like giving up, if he pushes through when he wants to quit, then he experiences the runner's high. So they say. I'll have to take their word for it.

This is what the Scripture says about our race. There's a runner's high to be had, but we have to run through the wall before we get there.

We don't have difficulties and challenges in our lives just because we're Christians. No one escapes life's hurts and disappointments and grief. The difference will be how we handle them and what comes out of them. Do we come out stronger, richer, wiser? Or beaten and defeated?

When running the race set before you, you will hit the wall. If you know the reality, then you'll know to feel encouraged when you hit the wall. Rejoice when you hit the wall. Consider it all joy when you hit the wall. The runner's high is just beyond. Empowered by Jesus, who is filling you with Himself, the wall will not hold you back. Can you imagine any circumstance for which Jesus is not enough? "What is impossible with men is possible with God" (Luke 18:27). "I am the LORD, the God of all mankind. Is anything too hard for me?" (Jeremiah 32:27–28).

No wall can stand against the onslaught of faith. Remember Jericho's walls? Huge, gigantic, scary-looking walls. They fell as if they were made of hay after the faithful kept marching in step with the Spirit's voice. When you hit the wall, keep going. One more step. Then one more step. Until the wall falls.

By describing our journey as a race, the Lord is reminding us that it's not a walk in the park. He is calling us to something that requires commitment, discipline, focus, and stamina. It requires decision. More than anything else, it requires surrender.

FULL SURRENDER

"Surrender?" you might be thinking. "Surrender sounds passive and weak. You need to be strong to run a long-distance race."

We are confronted again with the dichotomy of the *altared* life. My weakness makes way for His strength. My surrender makes way for His power. "What is impossible with men is possible with God" (Luke 18:27). To fully grasp the import of this statement, you have to accept both halves.

What is impossible with man.... You have to come to the realization that it is impossible for you to run the race on your own power. Your intentions are good. You know a lot of doctrine and have memorized a lot of Bible verses. You are absolutely determined to walk in victory. But your experience is failure, start again, a little victory, failure, start again.... The day comes when you say, "What a wretched man I am! Who will rescue me from this body of death?" (Romans 7:24–25). The word translated "wretched" means suffering, afflicted, miserable.

Have you ever thought, *I'd be happier if I weren't a Christian. I'd be happier if I could just chuck it all and not care. I wish I could just not believe! It makes me miserable!* I've been right there. *O miserable woman that I am*, I've thought. *How can I shed the dead weight of my own feeble efforts and get somewhere? I wish I just didn't care!* We have to come to a place of knowing with great certainty that the life we seek is impossible in the power of even the most devoted believer.

Once we've come to the end of ourselves, we can embrace the second part of Jesus's statement, "What is impossible with men *is possible with God*" (emphasis mine). We begin to live in that *altared* state we have been discussing. Surrendered, available, His. There is a way of ordering your inner life so that you are always bowed before Him, a living offering. He is the initiator, the living voice, the stirrer-into-action. When you find yourself out of position, your flesh rising up and taking over, you just return to Him. You don't spend time beating up yourself. You just admit sin, return to the altar. You say, "This is how I am when I'm not *altared*. Apart from You, I can do nothing." Little by little, the altar becomes the place where your soul is most at home.

Instead of the grueling walk of duty, you find yourself delighting in the discipline and gladly choosing the ways of the Spirit. You embrace the difficulties that are working perseverance into your character. You find that the inner position of surrender eliminates the power outer circumstances have to throw you off your stride.

Run with perseverance the race set out for you, relying on the indwelling power of Him who called you.

Missionary Bertha Smith, a missionary to China during the early 1900s, tells of a transforming realization. She found that the victory she so desired to experience was beyond her ability to effect. "Not knowing how to walk in the Spirit," she wrote in *Go Home and Tell*, "I was often filled today and empty tomorrow." She describes the change in her life when she fully realized that Christ lived in her and would express Himself through her. "I came into the glorious Bible truth that Christ lives in me. Joyous release! No longer did I have to strive for victory over self, the world, and the devil, but just to act on the fact that Christ was my victory and ... 'Let go and let God.'"

In her newly sharpened realization of Christ's indwelling life, she studied 2 Corinthians 9:8: "And God is able to make all grace abound toward you, that you, always having all sufficiency in all things, may have an abundance for every good work" (KJV).

Each word had significance for her. For example, here are a few of her notes that grabbed my heart:

Able — He is the all-powerful One who spoke the universe into existence. Certainly he is able to do for me all that I can ever need.

Abound — There would not be just enough strength, wisdom, and patience to get by, but abundance that could never give out.

To every good work — Why is such abundant grace given to me? Is it that I sometimes may do a little service for him? It is that I may *always* serve him! How? Am I just to serve in my own human weakness? No! I "always having all sufficiency in all things, may abound to every good work."

Smith concludes with these words: "Such a victorious, abundant life should only be the normal life for one in whom Christ himself [is] actually living."

Deeper surrender, more power, abounding in good works. *Altared* living, the key to victory.

THE POWER TO RECREATE DESIRE

"It is God who works in you to will and to act according to his good purpose" (Philippians 2:13).

God works in you to will His good purpose. He works *in* you, not just on you, or for you, or with you. In you. His power working in you is recreating your desires so that they match His. He works in you so that you actively want what He wants for you. He is freeing you so that His purposes and yours become the same.

This inner work, accomplished by His power, is landscaping your soul. Tilling the soil, pulling up the old rooted plants, bringing in new topsoil, planting, watering, weeding, waiting for the plants to take root, fertilizing. A careful and prolonged process.

I have just had a garden put in at my house. When I first decided to do this, I thought someone would come one day and dig some holes and put in some plants and—*voila*! A garden! Much to my surprise it has been a long and drawn-out project. Much messier for much longer than I intended. Even now, it looks kind of scraggly. At the moment, instead of enhancing the landscape, it mars the landscape. But I've come too far to turn back. They tell me it will root and flower and be lush and beautiful soon.

When God landscapes your soul, it is not a quick and tidy project. It's often messy. It requires the old soil to be tilled up. The soul-landscaper says, "Break up your unplowed ground" (Jeremiah 4:3). The seed has to fall on prepared soil or it won't put down roots. Breaking up the unplowed ground is indeed a dirty job.

God refers to His Word as a seed that falls into the ground and either takes root or dies. It all depends on the state of the soil.

Life Unhindered!

God may be using circumstances or people in your life to turn over the topsoil. You may feel as though the life you worked so hard to keep smooth and presentable is being ripped up and destroyed. Maybe you've resisted the process. Maybe you keep trying to smooth it over and make it look like it used to, but to no avail. If you will surrender yourself to your heart's Plowman, you will see that you are being prepared to produce a harvest.

Is there some pulling up going on? Some breaking up of fallow ground? Some digging and planting and watering and fertilizing? Are you in the messy phase of the project?

Your life is becoming like a watered garden. Your life is about to be lush with the Spirit's fruit. Your heart is being so completely excavated that it will be like new. It is being replanted with the living Word, which is taking root and growing fruit. The heart wants what it wants, they say. Let the power of the living, indwelling, present Jesus renovate your heart so when your heart wants what it wants, it wants what He wants.

It is God working in you to will His good purpose. What is His good purpose? What did He pour out all of heaven's Treasure to accomplish? He wants the world to be brought to the saving knowledge of His Son. As He reworks your life, making you a watered garden, displaying His fruit in your life, He is creating in you a heart that longs for a hurting world to meet a loving Savior. Every work He does in you has one goal: to be present through you to a hurting, dying world.

THE POWER TO ENERGIZE

"It is God who works in you . . . to act according to his good purpose" (Philippians 2:13).

There is a word play in this sentence. The word translated "works" and the word translated "act" is the same Greek word. The word is *energeo* and it means to work actively and with energy; to be effective. The subject of the verb in both cases ascribes the action to God. He works *in you* to work *through you*.

His first inner work is to realign your passions and mold them to match His. Then, from that work, comes the spontaneous overflow of your heart's desires into your actions. It's a process. It comes together progressively. God works your recreation from the inside to the outside.

Many of our actions and behaviors are so ingrained and automatic that it takes much retraining to get them on track with the new heart. Our responses, our reactions, our impressions—all those things that happen without intention and planning—they are all on automatic pilot. The brain is set up to handle many things automatically. Let me describe how a response becomes automatic.

The brain is made up of billions of nerve cells called neurons. These neurons communicate information to each other over neural pathways that are established by repeated use. When one neuron passes on information to the next, a connection is formed called a synapse. For any response, a message has to have passed from neuron to neuron, forming connections (synapses) as it goes, until it culminates in an action. It is a chain reaction. Like dominoes falling.

If an action is performed only once, the synapse is weak and may disintegrate. If, however, the action is performed over and over, the synapses grow stronger each time and soon there is a well-worn path in the brain whose connections are likely permanent. It's a process kind of like when you get in your car and start to drive to church, but suddenly find that you are headed toward your office instead. In your brain, there are well-worn paths that you automatically travel without thinking. So, whatever triggers the first neuron puts the synaptic connection in motion and without any deliberate thought, the whole train of neurons is activated and you are acting in a way that seems automatic. If, however, the neural path is left unused for a time, the connections weaken and, in some cases, disappear.

Let me illustrate how this works. Have you ever watched a baby learn to walk? First, there's crawling, scooting, and cruising. Along the way, synapses have been forming and strengthening. Now comes the big show. Walking. Remember how wobbly he is in the beginning? He keeps trying, each time strengthening the synapses involved, until you turn around and he's moved on to running. For a time he has to concentrate on every muscle movement, balance with caution, think about every movement. But eventually the neural cells required for walking have formed strong enough synapses that he never has to think about walking again. In fact, if he tries now to concentrate on the movements involved in walking, he couldn't describe them. Once the synapses have formed, autopilot kicks in.

In many cases the responses we have to situations and people—fear, anger, defensiveness, hurt—have become automatic. From early on our brains have constructed well-connected synaptic pathways that are triggered automatically.

When we understand how God designed our brains, then we can see again how He has made us healable. Again we realize that God designed and created everything so that it is useful to Him in accomplishing His purposes.

Healing works like this. You have a response that is automatic. To you, it feels like the natural and correct response to the situation. It just happens. As you let God do His deep work in you, you begin to realize that perhaps those responses are, after all, not appropriate, even sinful. But what can you do? By the time you realize it, the well-used chain of synapses has already fired and before you can make any other decision, you have already spoken, or acted, or spiraled into a familiar emotional state.

For example, Mary's mother was a perfectionist. The way that she loved Mary was by trying to make her perfect, but it came out as constant criticism. Mary learned to be afraid to try anything new. She could "hear" the criticism in advance. As a grown-up, Mary thought she heard criticism in many comments and was touchy and defensive. She alienated most people. She had a well-traveled neural pathway in her brain: she heard a question and that activated her defensiveness pathway. By the time the person had finished her sentence, Mary was a long way down the road toward anger. She responded as if the person had insulted her and accused her of being incompetent. Mary believed that to be true. She believed her response was exactly proportional to the situation. As she began to heal, she recognized that even though the responses felt right to her, she was really traveling a well-worn but deceitful synaptic pathway. She began to work hard to catch herself—even when she had already gone some distance down that road—and act in a new way. The new way felt false and unfamiliar, but she persisted. Little by little, she created a new synaptic pathway and the old road—left untraveled—gradually is disappearing. Her new normal is walking in the truth.

Remember, as a new creation in Christ, you now have a will that can freely choose against sin. This process will take time and be messy, but God has built the healing potential into your structure. You are healable, built to heal.

Synaptic paths are strengthened by use. If they are not used, the synapses begin to weaken and will eventually disappear. When you recognize a situation that triggers one of your automatic sinful responses, you can start building a new synaptic pathway. It will be awkward and take concentration and conscious reliance on the power of God working in you to act according to His good pleasure. It will be like a baby learning to walk, but you can know that every time you deliberately choose the Spirit-led response, the new synaptic connections are getting stronger and the old ones weaker. In time, the new way will be the automatic response. It will become the holy highway instead of the path for sin to travel. "The highway of the upright avoids evil; he who guards his way guards his life" (Proverbs 16:17).

Author Julie Morris tells her story about letting go of old patterns and finding freedom in her book *Guided By Him:*

"You're stupid!" "You're fat!" "You're lazy!" These words hurled at me growing up left me with scars far more disfiguring than ones that are just skin deep.

Because I was bombarded by so much criticism, I lived in a constant state of fear. I worried about everything! But when I was only five or six, I found a safe place where I could go—the refrigerator! Eating always calmed my nerves and distracted me from my fears.

When I got older, my problem with stress-eating got worse. Even though I was the RN supervisor of a large medical-surgical floor at a hospital, telling people what to do to get healthy, I couldn't lose the pounds that made my blood pressure soar. I woke up every morning and pleaded with God to help me eat right that day. Every night I fell asleep promising to do better and praying that God would forgive me for eating in such an unhealthy way.

"Why do I continue to overeat if I want to lose weight more than anything in my life?" I asked myself. Something compelled me to do what I had just determined not to. In almost everything else I was in control—I knew what I wanted to do and did it—but with food it was different.

I continued to call out for God's help and finally began to make progress when I discovered practical instructions in the Bible that would help me to draw closer to Jesus and cooperate with him as—together—we dealt with my problems, one day at a time.

The discipline of spending these few minutes every day with the Lord has been life-changing. I lost my extra pounds over 25 years ago and have kept them off! And God has changed weaknesses to strengths and my misery to ministry.

With God's help, Julie worked hard to rewire the synaptic pathways in her brain. She found freedom from a lifelong destructive pattern, and now reaches out to lead others to that freedom through her Step Forward weight-loss programs. She is not set free just so she will be healthier and more disciplined, but so that she can pass that freedom on.

When we use our will to will God's will we can let go of old patterns that kept us isolated. We can be the vehicles through which God can unleash His Spirit in the world. We can lead people with integrity and courage, instead of responding to others out of our own woundedness. We can become healers and encouragers, engaged in our culture and courageous in our calling.

$\mathscr{D}$iscussion

1. Why do you think the writer of Hebrews calls the Christian life a race?

2. How does God develop stamina in us?

3. How do past experiences and memories hinder us? How did God design our brains to be healable?

4. Review the concepts and identify insights that relate to some or all the four characteristics of fully free people.

   • Be vehicles through which God's Spirit will be unleashed in the world.

   • Be leaders of influence and uncompromised integrity.

   • Be courageous in their calling and engaged in their culture.

   • Be passionate about God as they step out and take risks together with other believers.

CHAPTER 8

His Power Through You

He works in you to work through you. The very work that He does inside you will find expression outside you, through you. You have been put into relationship with exactly those people whose lives will be enriched by the work God does through you.

> *"If anyone is thirsty, let him come to me and drink. Whoever believes in me, as the Scripture has said, streams of living water will flow from within him." By this he meant the Spirit, whom those who believed in him were later to receive.*
> —John 7:37–39

Living water in, living water out. What Jesus pours into us, He pours out through us. The Holy Spirit, the Spirit of Christ in us, is the living water.

Jesus called these words out loudly at the high point of the Feast of Tabernacles. The Feast was a joyous occasion, held in the Temple area in Jerusalem, with Jews from everywhere gathered for the annual weeklong celebration. John says that Jesus spoke these words "on the last and greatest day of the Feast" (John 7:37). The celebration on that day, known as the water pouring ceremony, was a beautiful pageant of music and dancing and concluded with the water pouring. Everyone's thoughts were on the coming Messiah, and emotions were stirred. At the crescendo of the celebratory festivities, water was poured out from a golden pitcher at the foot of the altar in the Temple courtyard. In this setting Jesus cried out offering living water to His hearers.

The festival represents the people's experience in the wilderness. The whole weeklong Feast of Tabernacles was a celebration of God's faithfulness to their forefathers while they wandered in the wilderness and lived in tents (tabernacles). The water pouring ceremony commemorates when water gushed from a rock in the desert. When there was no sign of water, no hope of water, water came from the least likely place. A rock.

Jesus is both the rock and the water that flows from the rock. He is a pourer-outer. When He comes into our lives, then He comes through our lives.

When we come to Jesus to receive all from Him, He pours Himself out in us to pour Himself out through us to those around us. Hudson Taylor once wrote, "If you are ever drinking at the Fountain, with what will your life be running over? Jesus, Jesus, Jesus!"

> But we have this treasure in jars of clay to show that this all-surpassing power is from God and not from us. We are hard pressed on every side, but not crushed; perplexed, but not in despair; persecuted, but not abandoned; struck down, but not destroyed.
> —2 Corinthians 4:7–10

He calls us to be the containers of His life. The fact that His transforming power can come through even a jar of clay proves that His power is the power. It doesn't matter what vessel holds it. The power is the power.

When we can be hard pressed, but not crushed; perplexed, but not in despair; persecuted, but not abandoned; struck down, but not destroyed—then we are containers and dispensers of a power not our own. When there is nothing that looks like power, but power comes through anyway—it is clearly an all-surpassing power that is from God and not from us.

BROKEN VESSELS

Use your imagination with me again. Imagine a clay pot. Clay pots are easily broken or cracked. They're not very sturdy. Imagine this clay pot all cracked, with pieces broken out of it. Not attractive. Not valuable. Ready for the trash heap.

Now imagine water pouring into that clay pot. What happens? The water pours out through the broken places. If water keeps on pouring in, then water will keep on pouring out.

If your goal was for the pot to hold the water, then it would have been a poor choice. But if your goal was for the pot to pour the water out, then you couldn't have found a more perfect pot.

My friend, author Diane Dike, suggests another picture with our broken, cracked clay pot. Diane suggests turning it on its side and looking inside. All dark in there. Except where the cracks and the broken places are. There the light shines through. The brokenness is where the glory can be seen.

Is this what Paul meant when he wrote these words?

"'My grace is sufficient for you, for my power is made perfect in weakness.' Therefore I will boast all the more gladly about my weaknesses, so that Christ's power may rest on me. That is why, for Christ's sake, I delight in weaknesses, in insults, in hardships, in persecutions, in difficulties. For when I am weak, then I am strong" (2 Corinthians 12:9–10).

Imagine! Who could have seen it coming? When Jesus made His home in the lives of human beings, He sought out broken pots. "It is not the healthy who need a doctor, but the sick. I have not come to call the righteous, but sinners" (Mark 2:17).

Do you have cracks and scars and gaping holes? You are just the kind of clay jar Jesus can pour Himself out through.

BEAUTIFUL WOUNDS

At the places where we have been broken, there the power of Christ is on display. I wrote the following in my book *He Restores My Soul* as I reflected on why Jesus's perfect resurrected body retained its scars.

How often our pride ... causes us to think of our wounds and our scars as something to hide; something ugly;

something demeaning; something that lessens our value. But look at Jesus. Look at what Jesus thought of His wounds: "Here, Thomas. Look at My wounds. Touch My scars. These are proof of My resurrection. I bear the marks of death, but I am alive!" Jesus knew His wounds were beautiful....

At the places where I am broken, the power of Christ is authenticated in me for others. Where I have submitted to the crucifixion, the power of the resurrection is on display. I can say, "Look at my wounds. Touch my scars. I have death-wounds, but I am alive." I can wear my wounds without shame. They tell a resurrection story.

Some places we are broken and wounded because life has dealt harsh blows. Other places we are broken because we have surrendered our self-life to the power of the Cross. We've let our self-life go so that we can experience the power of His resurrection in our lives.

The Cross has always been God's centerpiece. As we surrender on a daily, even minute-by-minute basis to the power of the Cross, we can say with Paul: "I have been crucified with Christ and I no longer live, but Christ lives in me. The life I live in the body, I live by faith in the Son of God, who loved me and gave himself for me.... May I never boast except in the cross of our Lord Jesus Christ, through which the world has been crucified to me, and I to the world" (Galatians 2:20; 6:14). Every place in your life that bears a crucifixion wound is an opening for the power of the indwelling Christ to be put on display. The wounds of crucifixion are beautiful to behold.

LIVE CRUCIFIED

We're back to *altared* living again. It's the key to everything. All the power, all the provision, all the fullness, all the abundance. It all flows from surrender.

How do you translate this principle into real-time living? How do you move this from being heady theology to being applicable to daily life?

Let me introduce you to what I call "crucifixion moments." Every time you recognize that the habits of your old life have surfaced, or some hint of your flesh is raising its ugly head, you have come to a crucifixion moment. A moment of choice. Surrender immediately to the power of the Cross or strengthen those ties to your old life.

Every time you encounter a crucifixion moment, it is an opportunity either to live in the *altared* state or climb down off the altar and meddle. It is a mental decision. You recognize the old life's pull, the ease of the familiar synaptic pathways. You know where it's about to take you. You've been down this road a thousand times at least. You know it is a dead end.

Stop. Decide. I say to myself, "No, in the name of Jesus." Don't do the act. Don't say the word. Don't dwell on the thought. Move on. Or, maybe crucifying your old ways means taking some action rather than avoiding it. Say what needs to be said instead of being afraid of rejection. Do something to reach out in love instead of letting someone else handle it.

Leave the situation in His hands. You stay crucified. Little by little, the old well-worn ways are losing their grip on you. New pathways are strengthening their synapses and taking the place of your old life. Old things are passing away, new things are coming into being.

Welcome crucifixion. It is the only way to experience the power of resurrection. Be on the lookout for the opportunities to let flesh die. Get it out of the way.

For example: Imagine that you've been saving money for something you really want. New furniture, or a new car, maybe. A family in the community has just lost everything to a fire. They are in desperate need of immediate financial help. The Lord is prompting you to give that money you've been saving to the family in need. Crucifixion moment.

Or imagine this: You have a busy day ahead. Deadlines, errands, phone calls to return, emails to answer. A woman calls. You know her only slightly. She is in your Sunday School class. You have never had a conversation of any depth with her. It's not like she's your good friend. But she was just told that she has breast cancer, and she's all alone. Crucifixion moment.

Imagine this: Your co-worker often makes mistakes and it's up to you to correct them. Her mistakes double your workload. She just made another mistake. Your impulse is to belittle her and scold her. You know she is already embarrassed that she can't seem to catch on to the job. Crucifixion moment.

Imagine that years ago you had a falling-out with a friend. You haven't spoken in many years. Bitterness has grown over time. She thinks you're wrong, and you think she's wrong. The Living Word speaks to your heart: "Seek peace and pursue it" (1 Peter 3:11). You know that obedience demands that you contact her and apologize and make every effort to restore the relationship. You flesh tries to bargain. "If I apologize and she doesn't, that's the end of it!" But the Spirit says, "Go against your flesh. Humble yourself and demand nothing in return." Crucifixion moment.

Do you see how it works? Everything that engages your flesh holds the potential for dying to flesh and experiencing the power of resurrection.

HIS POWER

God's power acts for you, in you, and through you. He has called you to run a race, and He has empowered you to obey that call. Your flesh holds you back. Your flesh hinders you. God is actively working to get rid of flesh, the old self-powered way of living. Have you every heard of a "fat flush"? Jesus is doing a "flesh flush."

His power is changing you from the inside out, pouring out through you at the broken places. Flowing from your crucifixion wounds.

As He works in you to heal you, it is so that you can reach out to others who are hurting. He has one reason for His indwelling power: so His power in you can be His power through you. He wants to touch your world through your personality, your gifts, your words, your actions.

"We proclaim him, admonishing and teaching everyone with all wisdom, so that we may present everyone perfect in Christ. To this end I labor, struggling with all *his energy*, which so powerfully works *in me*" (Colossians 1:28–29, emphasis mine).

Discussion

1. Why does God work tirelessly to heal and restore you?

2. Do you think that God has positioned you strategically so that the work He is doing in you will pour out to exactly those who need it?

3. At what points of brokenness do you see Christ working powerfully through you?

4. Review the concepts and identify insights that relate to some or all of the four characteristics of fully free people.

   - Be vehicles through which God's Spirit will be unleashed in the world.

   - Be leaders of influence and uncompromised integrity.

   - Be courageous in their calling and engaged in their culture.

   - Be passionate about God as they step out and take risks together with other believers.

Let us fix our eyes on Jesus, the
author and perfecter of our faith . . .

Key 4
His Presence

Face Up

*T*he writer previously had directed our attention to the lives of the faithful. Now he tells us to look away from them and stare fixedly at Jesus. Glance at the faithful forebears, but let your gaze come to rest on Jesus. Concentrate on Jesus.

"Let us fix our eyes on Jesus, the author and perfecter of our faith" (Hebrews 12:2). He is, after all, the one who initiated faith in them. He planted it and stirred it into life. He is the one who has inaugurated *your* faith. He is the one who calls it out of hiding and propels it into risk-taking action. He authors your faith, as He did theirs.

He not only gives faith its start, but He also brings it to completion. He perfects it, puts the finishing touches on it. He brings it into full flower. He is bringing *your* faith to fullness. The Greek word translated "perfect" means to reach a goal, to win the prize. Perhaps this is another way of calling Jesus "the Alpha and the Omega, the Beginning and the End" (Revelation 21:6). The Author and the Perfecter.

Fix your eyes on Jesus. Lock your gaze on Him. Everything else can be perceived correctly if His presence is the reference point.

Your mind always needs a reference point to correctly see reality. For example, imagine that you see a photograph of an object and the object fills the frame. It looks big. Then you see a photograph of that same object, but held in a person's hand. Now, with the hand as a reference point, your perception of the object's size changes. Or, imagine that you are in a traffic jam and all around you are big trucks that obscure your view of the horizon. If the trucks begin to move, it will feel as though you are the one moving. When your horizon comes back in view, you will reorient and know that you are sitting still. The horizon is your reference point. Without a reference point, your perceptions are skewed. Jesus invites us to make His presence our one and only reference point, the basis for our orientation. Fix your eyes on Him.

Do an experiment with me. Look around and find a single object to fasten your eyes on. Pick something about an arm's length away. Now stare fixedly at it for several seconds. What happens to your view of surrounding objects when your eyes are locked on a single object? Everything else is a little bit blurred and out of focus. That object on which you have fixed your attention is clear and focused. When we get our eyes locked on Jesus, His presence is our reality. Nothing else seems so compelling or so worthy of attention. His face fills our frame of reference and everything else pales.

When you are running the race marked out for you, look at Jesus. Don't focus on your own progress. Don't focus on other runners. Don't measure how far you've come or how far you have to go. Look at Jesus.

As a child, Rebekah Naylor heard God's call to be a missionary and a doctor. The first woman to graduate from the surgical residency program at University of Texas Southwestern Medical School, she became a surgeon, moved in 1974 to Bangalore Baptist Hospital in India, and served there for an amazing period of 35 years. In addition to her pressing medical duties, she started a choir, taught Bible studies, led chapels, supervised building projects, and created a strategy to reach India through the hospital's ministry.

The hospital's current director, Alexander Thomas, shares the difficulties Naylor faced, "Living alone on the hospital campus often meant being the only doctor on call and having to deal not only with surgical problems but also medical, obstetrical, and administrative problems. As if that were not enough, she had intermittent resident-visa and medical-license problems. Through all of this she never forgot her calling. She coped admirably. She became an example for others—an example difficult to follow."

Recently retired, Dr. Naylor reflected on her ministry. Asked what it felt like to be, at one time, the only Southern Baptist missionary serving in a population approaching one billion people, her response focused on the provision of God.

"I focused on my work and the individuals whom I helped physically and spiritually to be whole. If I thought about all of India and me being one person, it would have been overwhelming. I also claimed God's promise that His resources are enough. He has a plan for a way that all the peoples of India could hear about Jesus."

Dr. Naylor knew that what God had called her to do, He would empower her for. With Jesus as her reference point, she could give herself fully, unhindered.

HIS PRESENCE WITH HIS PEOPLE

God's presence has always been crucial for His people, and He has always made His presence known. Moses refused to move without God's presence: "If your Presence does not go with us, do not send us up from here. How will anyone know that you are pleased with me and with your people unless you go with us? What else will distinguish me and your people from all the other people on the face of the earth?" (Exodus 33:15–16).

What distinguishes God's people from all the other people on the face of the earth? His presence.

From the beginning, God has revealed His presence. The opening words of Scripture declare as fact the presence of God, "In the beginning God...." The first humans walked with God and knew His presence, apparently in a way that their physical senses could perceive. The punishment for the first sin sent them away from the intimacy of His presence as they had known it before. From then on, the Lord revealed Himself in various ways until He fully revealed Himself in Jesus. "In the past God spoke to our forefathers through the prophets at many times and in various ways, but in these last days he has spoken to us by his Son" (Hebrews 1:1–2).

When God led the children of Israel out of Egypt, His presence never left them. He revealed His presence in a form they could see to give them assurance on their journey. "By day the LORD went ahead of them in a pillar of cloud to guide them on their way and by night in a pillar of fire to give them light, so that they could travel by day or night. Neither the pillar of cloud by day nor the pillar of fire by night left its place in front of the people" (Exodus 13:21–22).

Every step of the way, the presence of the Lord was visible. The cloud of the Lord's presence is a thread that runs through the narrative of the people's travels through the wilderness. Even though they were in the wilderness 40 years because of their own rebellion, still God never left them.

> *In all the travels of the Israelites, whenever the cloud lifted from above the tabernacle, they would set out; but if the cloud did not lift, they did not set out—until the day it lifted. So the cloud of the LORD was over the tabernacle by day, and fire was in the cloud by night, in the sight of all the house of Israel during all their travels.*
> —Exodus 40:36–38

His presence was their reference point.

HIS PRESENCE IN HIS PEOPLE

His presence with His people was only the precursor. He was preparing them for the day when His presence would be in them. He started setting the stage during the wilderness years. He instructed them to build a tabernacle to be His dwelling place. "I will put my dwelling place among you" (Leviticus 26:11). God dwelt among His people—inside them, in the center of them, in the heart of them. His dwelling place was first portrayed as a physical tabernacle (dwelling place or tent). When they encamped in a location, the people were to set up the Tabernacle first. Then they were to set up their own tents around its perimeter. The dwelling place of God was inside His people.

The Tabernacle pointed to a reality that was consummated in Jesus. When Jesus put on flesh, the Scripture describes it this way: "The Word became flesh and made his dwelling among us" (John 1:14). John, steeped in Hebrew Torah, was no doubt directly borrowing phrasing from God's promise to His people in the wilderness. Jesus lived for 33 years in a body of flesh, dwelling among His people. But still, this was not the final act. God had always planned to indwell His people. He had always been laying the groundwork for the grand finale.

Jesus, talking of the Holy Spirit, who is also called the Spirit of Christ, said of Him: "He lives *with* you and will be *in* you" (John 14:17, emphasis mine). At that time, before Jesus was resurrected and ascended to the Father, the Spirit was present, but He was present *with*. Jesus said that soon He would be present *in*.

Examine this passage recorded in John when Jesus, hours from crucifixion, was promising His disciples that they would always have His presence.

> *"And I will ask the Father, and he will give you another Counselor to be with you forever—the Spirit of truth. The world cannot accept him, because it neither sees him nor knows him. But you know him, for he lives with you and will be in you. I will not leave you as orphans; I will come to you. Before long, the world will not see me anymore, but you will see me. Because I live, you also will live. On that day you will realize that I am in my Father, and you are in me, and I am in you. Whoever has my commands and obeys them, he is the one who loves me. He who loves me will be loved by my Father, and I too will love him and show myself to him."*
> —John 14:16–21

Jesus promises them "another Counselor." What does He mean? Another one to take Jesus's place because Jesus won't be present any longer? Is His time up so He's going to send someone else? Let's see what Jesus says about that. Let's compare the way He talks about the Holy Spirit and about Himself.

Holy Spirit	Jesus
The world neither sees Him or knows Him	In a little while, the world will not see Jesus
But you know Him	You will see Jesus; Jesus will show Himself to you
He lives with you and will be in you	Jesus will come to you; He will be in you

Jesus says that He will not leave them orphaned. He will come to them. "Because I live, you will also live." What is He saying? The Greek word translated "live" is a form of the word *zoe*, which usually means the supernatural, spiritual life. A different word, *bios*, is most often used to mean biological life. Jesus means more than biological life. In each of these representative statements, the Greek word for "life" is a form of *zoe*.

> *"I am the way and the truth and the life."* —John 14:6

> *"I am the resurrection and the life."* —John 11:25

> *"So that they may take hold of the life that is truly life."* —1 Timothy 6:19

There are many other statements about life, abundant life eternal life, and the Life Himself that reinforce this reality. Jesus is saying that because He has supernatural, eternal, resurrection life, *therefore* His disciples will have supernatural, eternal, resurrection life. Why? Because He will be *in them*, imparting His life to them, living His life through them. "On that day you will realize that... I am in you."

"God has given us eternal life, and this life is *in his Son*. He who has the Son has life; he who does not have the Son of God does not have life" (1 John 5:11–12, emphasis mine). The *zoe* is in Jesus—not something He gives, but something He is. The one who "has" Jesus has *zoe*. Why? Because Jesus is in that one, and *zoe* is in Jesus.

Add one more statement that Jesus makes in this discourse with His disciples."If anyone loves me, he will obey my teaching. My Father will love him, and *we* will come to him and make *our* home with him" (John 14:23, emphasis mine).

Another Comforter. Like I have a sister, and I have another sister. One doesn't take the place of the other. So, yes, the Holy Spirit has come to dwell in us, but Jesus Himself is also in us. Jesus says that the *Holy Spirit*, who is just exactly like Jesus, and the *Father*, who is just exactly like Jesus, and *Jesus*, who is just exactly like the Father and like the Spirit, will make *Their* home in you. (See Hebrews 1:3). Triune God, Three-One God, will make His home in you. Three in such perfect harmony that they are one. "I am in my Father, and you are in me, and I am in you."

I often use the following example, based on my understanding of Scripture, to illustrate the triune nature of the God who has made His home in us. Imagine that I have the most wonderful thoughts in all the world, and if you knew my thoughts, you would be transformed by them. How would I communicate my thoughts to you? I would use words. When I translate my thoughts into words, then my thoughts and my words are exactly the same thing in two different forms. Just alike. Yet it would take one other element for me to communicate my thoughts to you. It would take the breath of my mouth rushing over my vocal cords to create the voice that would carry my words to your ears. Three elements acting in such perfect harmony that they are one: thought (Father), word (Son), voice (Spirit).

God is not trapped in time and space and not subject to the laws of location. Jesus can be at the Father's right hand in the heavenlies and in you. The Father can be on the universe's throne and in you. The Spirit can be active in the heavenly realms and in you.

Do you believe that the Holy Spirit can be active in me, and in you, and in millions of believers at one time? Do you believe that Jesus can be working in my life, and in your life, and in the lives of millions of believers at one time? That God the Father can be working in millions of situations all over the planet at the same time? Of course you do. The eternal God is not limited to the laws of geography.

The point I want you to see is that the Scripture makes much of the fact that Jesus—in whom all the fullness of the Deity lives (Colossians 2:9)—lives in you. *In* you. John 15 picks up on the same conversation we've been looking at: "Remain in me, and I will remain in you.... I am the vine; you are the branches. If a man remains in me and I in him, he will bear much fruit; apart from me you can do nothing" (John 15:5, 45). And John writes later: "We know that we live in him and he in us, because he has given us of his Spirit" (1 John 4:13). Christ dwells in our hearts through faith (see Ephesians 3:17).

Jesus is no longer present in His physical body, but He is present through His Spirit. His presence in Spirit form in us is more effective for guiding, providing, protecting, teaching, and correcting. The very same Jesus who was, and the very same Jesus who is to come, is living His present-tense life in you right now.

On the third morning after His crucifixion, the Lord Jesus Christ rose from the dead and appeared to His disciples. He instructed them for some forty days and then ascended to the Father. On the first day of Pentecost He returned, not this time to be *with them* externally— clothed with that sinless humanity that God had prepared for Him, being conceived of the Holy Spirit in the womb of Mary—but now to be *in them* imparting *to them* His own divine nature, clothing Himself with *their* humanity, so that they each became "members in particular" of a new, corporate body through which Christ expressed Himself to the world of their day. He spoke with their lips. He worked with their hands. This was the miracle of new birth and this remains the very heart of the gospel!

—Major W. Ian Thomas, *The Saving Life of Christ*

Can you identify with Paul's words from Galatians 2:20? "I have been crucified with Christ and I no longer live, but Christ lives in me. The life I live in the body, I live by faith in the Son of God, who loved me and gave himself for me."

Do you believe that Jesus clothes Himself in your humanity? As you run the race set out for you, lean on Jesus. Let Him exert all His power through you. Nothing that God calls on you to do is possible in your own abilities. Only, *only* by the power of the living indwelling Jesus. The life you live in your body—live it by surrender to the present Jesus.

Don't ask, "What would Jesus do?" That implies He's not here. He is here! Ask, "Jesus, what are You doing? Do it through me." Speak through me. Respond through me. Think through me. Act through me.

Do you need to respond in love to a situation instead of in anger that comes naturally? Do you need just the right words to communicate love and encouragement? Do you need the energy to carry out one more task? Do you need compassion when your own response is resentment? Just breathe the name: *Jesus*. Live in an attitude of surrender to Him and a vital awareness of His life in you. Mentally, stand back. Get out of the way. Say to the living, indwelling Jesus, "I must decrease and You must increase."

Practice being aware of the living and present Jesus in you all the time. His power is not reserved for crises, or traumas, or moments of high drama. He is always, always in you. Practice staying *altared* so that the life of Jesus can freely flow through you every moment of every day.

EXPERIENCING HIS PRESENCE

Indwelling had always been the plan. As the Lord progressively unfolded the truth, revealing it over time, little by little, it all led up to the astounding finale. The fullness of salvation is Christ in you, the hope of glory. How does understanding the indwelling Christ move us toward freedom? How is Jesus in you setting you free?

First, He is setting you free of your own futile efforts toward holiness. "Apart from me, you can do nothing," Jesus said. On the other hand, "I can do all things through Christ who strengthens me." As you learn how to rest in Him, trusting every minute to His power working in you and through you, you are being set free of the cycle of failure and guilt.

He is training you to live in the awareness of His indwelling presence. Let Him remind you in your first waking thoughts: "I have clothed Myself in you." As you face challenges through the day, surrender to Jesus in you. "Jesus, act through me, think through me, reason through me, speak through me." Is there anything you might encounter for which Jesus is not enough?

When you pray, the indwelling life of Christ changes everything. You are not trying to get the attention of a God who is far away. You don't have to devise rituals that will make your prayers reach a distantly located God. He has made His home in you. If you have ever said to yourself, "I don't feel like my prayers get past the ceiling," then I have good news for you. They don't have to go even that far. Christ in you is moving you to pray and reproducing His prayers in your heart. This is the very Jesus who said to the Father while standing at Lazarus's tomb: "I know that You always hear me."

From inside, He has direct access to your mind and understanding. He can speak so intimately that He makes direct deposits from His mind to yours. He can bypass all those barriers to communication that can interfere when messages come from the outside. His communication is so intimate that many times it feels like your own idea. He frees you from the struggle to hear Him or try to understand His will for you. You can be in unbroken fellowship and conversation with Him on the inside, even while all kinds of things are whirling around you on the outside.

Sometimes that fellowship may have your full attention. In fact, once you live in the awareness of His ever-presence, you will be intentional about turning your attention to Him at every opportunity. Stuck in traffic? Back of the line? Stuck doing a boring, mindless task? Instead of feeling frustrated and impatient, welcome the time to enjoy that fellowship with Jesus.

As you get more accustomed to living in that awareness, you will find that you can be doing certain tasks and still be having an intimate interaction with Jesus. Your brain is able to multitask very well. As I'm writing this, concentrating on words and ideas and flow, I am actively in conversation with Jesus. "Jesus, what do You want to communicate here? What words are You wanting to use?" And I trust that He is able to direct my thoughts and awaken new ideas. When I am listening to someone share a struggle with me, as I listen, I'm saying, "Jesus, what do You want to say?" Everything, everything, everything can be immediately turned over to Him. Everything that starts feeling like a weight, transfer to His shoulders. Every person you find hard to love, let Him love. His presence in you frees you from the burden of handling things on your own.

You can tell that I think in pictures. This is the picture I see with the eyes of my heart when I want to get out of His way and let Him handle something: There I am. Then here comes Jesus. Big, big Jesus. He stands in front of me, but like the cloud of His presence the Israelites knew so well, He is all around me. I am inside Him. Remember how Moses walked into the cloud? "Then Moses entered the cloud as he went on up the mountain" (Exodus 24:18). I might stick my head out and say to the enemy, who is trying his best to get me to follow my flesh's lead, "Take it up with Him."

Let these words live in you: "*I am in my Father*, and *you are in me*, and *I am in you*" (emphasis mine). The presence of Christ in you frees you from the traps your enemy sets, trying to get your flesh involved in things.

He's your life coach. Right there to give you direction and to lead you into productive living. He's there to guide every thought in the right direction. He's there to encourage every action, clean out every attitude, detoxify every memory. He's there to empower you for anything required of you. Do you ever notice the stickers that come on a new computer that says something like "Powered by Intel." You are "powered by Jesus." The more you learn to surrender to His presence in you, the more free you are.

Missionary Hudson Taylor discovered this secret some years into his ministry, and it changed him forever. He embraced Jesus's promise that anyone who thirsts can come to Him to drink and that, as a result, rivers of water would then flow out from one's innermost being.

Here is what Taylor wrote about this promise: "Can it be? Can the dry and thirsty one not only be refreshed—the parched soil moistened, the arid places cooled—but the land be so saturated that springs well up and streams flow down from it? Even so! And not mere mountain-torrents, full while the rain lasts, then dry again…but, 'from within shall flow rivers'— rivers like the mighty Yangtze, ever deep, ever full…. Always a stream, always flowing deep and irresistible!"

Living water does not stagnate. It flows with power and force. It flows out from you to those around you. What Jesus does inside you flows out from you to the world around you. A never-ending torrent of life-giving refreshment. Ministry that flows from duty or from good intentions or from guilt will never have the life-changing power of the living Jesus. Come to Him and drink. *Then*, rivers of living water will flow from your innermost being.

Discussion

1. Where is the presence of Jesus?

2. What does it mean to have Jesus as your reference point?

3. What is the ultimate purpose for His indwelling life?

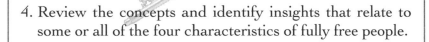

4. Review the concepts and identify insights that relate to some or all of the four characteristics of fully free people.

   • Be vehicles through which God's Spirit will be unleashed in the world.

   • Be leaders of influence and uncompromised integrity.

   • Be courageous in their calling and engaged in their culture.

   • Be passionate about God as they step out and take risks together with other believers.

CHAPTER 10

Restored

*A*s Jesus flows from our lives as Living Water, He is sweeping away everything that gets in the way or hinders the free flow of His life. Some hindrances are simply caught up in the mighty flow and washed out almost without effort. Other hindrances have deeper roots. They are being washed away bit by bit, eroded as the River flows. Either way, we can't have the River of Living Water flowing through us and be unchanged by His power. What He does in us flows out through us to the world around us. The more of our flesh He washes away, the more forcefully the River can flow.

God has a reason for filling us with Himself. That which He does in us, He then does through us.

> *All this is from God, who reconciled us to himself through Christ and gave us the ministry of reconciliation: that God was reconciling the world to himself in Christ, not counting men's sins against them. And he has committed to us the message of reconciliation. We are therefore Christ's ambassadors, as though God were making his appeal through us. We implore you on Christ's behalf: Be reconciled to God.*
> —2 Corinthians 5:18–20

Let Jesus do His mighty work in you so He can do His mighty work through you. Let Him restore your soul, so that you can reach out to others in the power of the Spirit, unhindered by flesh.

HE RESTORES MY SOUL

The living, indwelling Jesus is involved in a restoration project. From the time He makes you His home, He begins to restore your soul—your personality—bringing it to its intended purpose, which is to be a reflection of His glory. From inside, He is pouring Himself into your mind, your will, and your emotions.

Mind

> *The mind controlled by the Spirit is life and peace.*
> —Romans 8:6

> *Do not conform any longer to the pattern of this world, but be transformed by the renewing of your mind. Then you will be able to test and approve what God's will is—his good, pleasing and perfect will.*
> —Romans 12:2

> *We have the mind of Christ.*
> —1 Corinthians 2:16

> *Be made new in the attitude of your minds.*
> —Ephesians 4:23

> *No one knows the thoughts of God except the Spirit of God. We have not received…the Spirit who is from God, that we may understand what God has freely given us.*
> —1 Corinthians 2:11–12

Will

> *It is God who works in you to will and to act according to his good purpose.*
> —Philippians 2:13

"If you remain in me and my words remain in you, ask whatever you wish, and it will be given you."
—John 15:7

Emotions

God has poured out his love into our hearts by the Holy Spirit, whom he has given us.
—Romans 5:5

For Christ's love compels us.
—2 Corinthians 5:14

The powerful presence of Christ in you is recreating your desires to match His. From inside, He is pouring Himself into our personalities. Once He has access to our minds, then our minds are the control center for our will and our emotions. As He, from inside, washes our minds clean and deposits His thoughts into our minds, we are experiencing ever-increasing freedom. We can pick up the pace in the race set out for us to run.

I want to lay out in detail the process by which this inner transformation is happening. When we see this whole picture, it will be easier to yield to what God is doing in us. You will cooperate with the process instead of resisting it.

THE PROBLEM WITH FLESH

Often when the New Testament writers, especially Paul, use the word *flesh*, they mean the human nature acting on its own power, apart from the indwelling power of Christ. A non-believer has nothing but flesh. A believer, although she immediately has Christ indwelling her, still has pockets of flesh in her personality that remain active. Each of these leftover areas of flesh must be eradicated so that the power of Christ can take over what that flesh has been trying to control. *Sanctification* is the theological word for this process.

Flesh has to die. It can't be dressed up, or taught to act better, or improved upon. It is like a cancer. It doesn't belong in you. It can't be ignored. It is aggressive and invasive and it has to die.

Think of flesh as dead weight you carry around. Paul was describing the flesh that interfered with his desire to be holy when he wrote these words: "Who will rescue me from this body of death?" (Romans 7:24–25). Body of death—dead weight. It doesn't take much thought to realize that being freed of your remaining flesh will be like ridding yourself of weight and encumbrances. "The Spirit gives life; the flesh counts for nothing" (John 6:63). Flesh gets you nowhere.

I'm going to summarize a concept I addressed in great detail in my book *The Life-Changing Power in the Blood of Christ*. Remember the definition of *flesh* as we are using it right now: the human nature acting in its own power. Where did flesh first enter the picture? When the first humans acted on their own impulses, placing their own desires over the command of God. Here is the Scripture's definition of sin: "For all have sinned and fall short of the *glory* of God" (Romans 3:23, emphasis mine). Notice, it doesn't say we fall short of the standards, or of the expectations. We fall short of the glory. When Adam and Eve sinned, they fell short of the glory of God.

THE GLORY

What does the word *glory* mean? Its Hebrew root hints at "the outshining" or "the manifestation." The glory of God essentially means God manifested—God in a form you can see. The outshining. Let me illustrate. If you were looking at me right now, you would not be seeing me. You would be seeing the light rays that bounce off of me. You can't see me in the dark, because the only way to know what I look like is to see light rays bouncing off of me. You can't see me; you can only see my outshining. My glory, you might say.

The glory of God is His presence in a visible form. In the Old Testament it was the cloud. "Then the cloud covered the Tent of Meeting, and the *glory* of the LORD filled the tabernacle. Moses could not enter the Tent of Meeting because the cloud had settled upon it, and the *glory* of the LORD filled the tabernacle" (Exodus 40:34–35, emphasis mine). In the New Testament it is His Son. "The Son is *the radiance of God's glory* and the exact representation of his being" (Hebrews 1:3, emphasis mine).

Life Unhindered!

In the creation account in Genesis, God designed and created mankind to be His image (see Genesis 1:26). Mankind was to be the representation of His being. Mankind was to be the glory of God. God should have been able to point to humans and say, "Here is what I am like. Here is My representation in visible form." When the first sin occurred, mankind fell short of the glory of God.

From the beginning, God had a plan in place for how He would restore His glory to His people. He described it like this: "Christ in you, the hope of glory" (Colossians 1:27). It had always been the plan. It is still the plan. God will restore His glory in His people by indwelling them and transforming them from the inside out.

More pictures. The Scripture is very accommodating to those of us who think in pictures, because it is filled with visuals. Look again at the Tabernacle. Remember what God said about the Tabernacle?

> *"Then have them make a sanctuary for me, and I will dwell among them. Make this tabernacle and all its furnishings exactly like the pattern I will show you ... See that you make them according to the pattern shown you on the mountain."*
> —Exodus 25:8–9, 39–40

> *They serve at a sanctuary that is a copy and shadow of what is in heaven. This is why Moses was warned when he was about to build the tabernacle: "See to it that you make everything according to the pattern shown you on the mountain."*
> —Hebrews 8:4–5

His dwelling place, the Tabernacle, was to be made according to His specifications because the details had meaning. It was designed to disclose a reality. Its arrangement is not random.

When the Triune God created man in His image, I believe He created man to be a three-in-one being. Though there are other views, I am convinced we are made up of spirit—our vehicle for relating to God and the spiritual realm; soul—our vehicle for relating to each other and to the realm of thoughts and ideas; and body—our vehicle for relating to the physical realm. Though I am one coherent, unified person, I am made up of spirit, soul, and body. Some New Testament writers indicate this as they describe the nature of man.

> *May God himself, the God of peace, sanctify you through and through. May your whole spirit, soul and body be kept blameless at the coming of our Lord Jesus Christ.*
> —1 Thessalonians 5:23–24

> *For the word of God is living and active. Sharper than any double-edged sword, it penetrates even to dividing soul and spirit.*
> —Hebrews 4:12

The dwelling place that God instructed His people to build—the Tabernacle, later the Temple—is a triune dwelling place. The Tabernacle consists of the outer courtyard, which would correspond to our bodies; the sanctuary, which would correspond to our souls; and the Holy of Holies, the dwelling place of God—which corresponds to our spirits. When God commanded the people to build the Tabernacle, He was creating a prototype of the dwelling place He had in mind: His people.

> *Don't you know that you yourselves are God's temple and that God's Spirit lives in you? If anyone destroys God's temple, God will destroy him; for God's temple is sacred, and you are that temple.*
> —1 Corinthians 3:16–17

> *Do you not know that your body is a temple of the Holy Spirit, who is in you, whom you have received from God?*
> —1 Corinthians 6:19

> *For we are the temple of the living God.*
> —2 Corinthians 6:16

THE RESTORATION PROJECT

When God comes to take up residence in you, He makes His home in your spirit. That is His Holy of Holies. Immediately, His presence makes your spirit holy. But your soul—the sanctuary—is still full of leftover flesh and sin. He begins a restoration project, restoring your soul to its intended purpose. It is to be the place where His glory is displayed. In the Tabernacle, the glory of God in the form of a cloud would fill the sanctuary. God wants His glory to fill your soul. He wants your soul to be where His presence is made visible. He wants your personality to be restored to His image, so that you are the exact representation of His being. He wants to restore His glory.

How does this restoration happen? Remember that flesh has to die. It has to be crucified. "I am crucified with Christ," Paul said. What does that mean? Let me lay out several principles that will help you see the process.

1. Your flesh—your "old man" or your "old nature"—died in Christ's crucifixion. "For we know that our old self was crucified with him so that the body of sin might be done away with, that we should no longer be slaves to sin—because anyone who has died has been freed from sin" (Romans 6:6–7).

God, who is not limited to linear time, and who acts outside of time, included all your flesh in the crucifixion of the Son, who bore our sins in His body on the Cross. However, you and I can keep our old flesh on automatic life support. We can keep it acting alive, though it is dead.

Years ago there was a movie called *Weekend at Bernie's.* In the movie, two young executives were invited to their boss's beach house. Before they arrived, their boss was murdered by a mobster. The two young men pretend Bernie, their boss, is still alive. They move him around and get behind him to animate him so that he seems to be living. The whole movie is taken up with their deceit and the mobster's frustration trying to kill Bernie, who, of course, is already dead.

This silly movie plot reminds me of how we try to animate our flesh, even though it is dead. What hard work! Dragging around a body of death!

2. We are so used to letting our flesh have its way, that we often don't even recognize it for what it is. "That's just how I am," we say. It seems to be a real, living part of us. It's like phantom pain experienced by an amputee whose brain still believes it is getting signals from the body part that no longer exists.

3. These pockets of active flesh are located in your soul. Their sphere of operation is in your mind. Flesh is taking up space that the glory of God could be filling.

4. The death your flesh must die is a crucifixion. Each pocket of flesh has to be surrendered to the power of the Cross in a "crucifixion moment."

I referred earlier to "crucifixion moments." Let me explain in more detail. These pockets of flesh are active in your life. As you are more sensitized to the power of the living, indwelling Jesus, you recognize many reactions and behaviors that you thought of as normal—"just who I am"—are actually flesh in operation. Fear, envy, anger, irritation, pettiness, pride—just flesh working. Now when that flesh is activated, instead of acting in it without thinking—letting your synaptic pathways work unchallenged—you will have come to a crucifixion moment. A moment of choice. Like Jesus, you have to *choose* the crucifixion. You can act in that flesh pattern one more time and make the synaptic pathway stronger. Or you can surrender it to crucifixion, act in concert with the indwelling Jesus, and let the flesh pattern die.

Flesh has to hang on the cross for a while before it dies, but just keep surrendering it. When the flesh reaction rises up, choose to say, "That's just flesh. I die to that." And keep on in the Spirit. And when that same flesh flares up again, say, "That's just flesh. I die to that." And keep on in the Spirit.

What engages flesh? Circumstances and events in your life engage your flesh. This is by God's design. He allows and engineers circumstances and makes sure you cross paths with certain personality types that are guaranteed to engage your flesh. Why? So you can surrender it to crucifixion. He brings it out so you can choose the cross and die to the flesh. Live *altared* so you can live free.

Every time you surrender flesh to crucifixion, you are opening the way for resurrection. When the supernatural life—the *zoe*—of Jesus rushes in to fill the space left vacant by crucified flesh, the power of His resurrection is your new experience. His glory is on display where old, rotting flesh has been displaced. The power of His death works *in* you, so the power of His life can work *through* you.

> *We always carry around in our body the death of Jesus, so that the life of Jesus may also be revealed in our body. For we who are alive are always being given over to death for Jesus' sake, so that his life may be revealed in our mortal body. So then, death is at work in us, but life is at work in you.*
> —2 Corinthians 4:10–12

By His presence in you, He is restoring His glory. You are being set free from the dead weight of your flesh to live in the power of the Spirit. The more flesh that is displaced by glory, the more we can be what God has designed us to be. The more we live by God's design, the more we can be leaders of influence and integrity, engaging our culture courageously and taking risks as God calls us to do so. As the presence of Christ in us becomes the presence of Christ through us, we are the vehicles through which God's Spirit is unleashed in the world.

Hudson Taylor can again be our example. He was willing to give up everything to reach the lost in China, and through him, God's Spirit was unleashed in power. He made a statement that captures the truth of how flesh crucified makes way for God's glory: "At home, you can never know what it is to be absolutely alone, amidst thousands, everyone looking on you with curiosity, with contempt, with suspicion, or with dislike. Thus to learn what it is to be despised and rejected of men...and then to have the love of Jesus applied to your heart by the Holy Spirit...this is precious, this is worth coming for."

Discussion

1. What is God's purpose for living in His people?

2. How do you understand "flesh"?

3. What is God's restoration process?

4. Review the concepts and identify insights that relate to some or all of the four characteristics of fully free people.

   * Be vehicles through which God's Spirit will be unleashed in the world.

   * Be leaders of influence and uncompromised integrity.

   * Be courageous in their calling and engaged in their culture.

   * Be passionate about God as they step out and take risks together with other believers.

CHAPTER 11

Face Time

The Hebrew word for "presence" is literally "faces." Not just face, singular, but faces, plural. One face has many expressions, each communicating something different. Scientists have identified seven facial expressions that have the same meaning in every culture. These expressions are anger, happiness, disgust, contempt, surprise, fear, and sadness. Where words will not communicate, a face can.

The face is the most expressive part of us. We can communicate with our faces more revealingly than with words or tone of voice. I'm always fascinated by how much a great actor or actress can communicate by facial expression.

In our day of email, text messages, blogs, and even phones, many miscommunications arise because there is no face-to-face presence. The same words can be understood differently by different people. It takes a face to really communicate. We try to make up for the deficiency with emoticons—little symbols expressing the emotion we mean to communicate. It helps a little, but an emoticon is no substitute for a face.

The study of facial communication is an emerging science, sometimes referred to as "seeing the voice." A thought or emotion registers on the face before it is spoken. The face registers the true emotion, even if the words are meant to mask the emotion. Facial expressions convey meaning, and we all know a person can also learn to mask emotion on her face. But our true emotions always register on our faces, even if only fleetingly.

As Malcolm Gladwell writes, "When we experience a basic emotion, a corresponding message is automatically sent to the muscles of the face. That message may linger on the face for just a fraction of a second, or be detectable only if you attached electrical sensors to the face, but it's always there." ("The Naked Face," *The New Yorker*, August 2002).

So, the face can't lie. Facial expression is so real, so honest. When you want to be sure you are heard, or be sure your communication is clear, you want face time.

"The LORD would speak to Moses face to face, as a man speaks with his friend" (Exodus 33:11). When we read that statement it says something far beyond the words in the sentence. Face-to-face. It implies intimacy. It suggests an open and revealing relationship. It means access.

The presence of the Lord is His face to your face. It speaks of something beyond love. Beyond passion. It speaks of friendship. Real friendship. The kind of friendship where you can read one another's faces even without words.

"I have sought your *face* with all my heart; be gracious to me according to your promise" (Psalm 119:58, emphasis mine). "My heart says of you, 'Seek his face!' Your face, LORD, I will seek" (Psalm 27:8).

Seek His face. He invites you into His presence, to be before His face. In Psalm 91:1 the writer talks about dwelling in the "secret place of the Most High" (KJV). In Psalm 31:20, the secret place is identified as "the secret place of your presence." If someone invites you to his secret place, he'll have to tell you how to get there. You need a special invitation.

My house sits on a little road off the beaten path. The address doesn't show up on a GPS or online mapping service or any other locator. It is my secret place. The only way for you to get here is for me to tell you exact directions. I have to tell you to watch for the red barn, and then take the next right. The nature of a secret place is that it is hidden and private. You can call me. You can email me. You can text me. But if you want to see my face, I will have to tell you precisely how to find me.

The Father has invited you to the secret place of His presence. He has invited you to His face. He wants to communicate with you in ways that only His face can speak.

SHINING FACES

When Moses emerged from face time with the Lord, he was changed. The difference was so profound that it was reflected on his face. The skin on his face glowed so brightly that the change startled the Israelites. The effect of having been before the Lord's face was evident to observers.

When we are face-to-face with the Lord, we are changed. We are changed in profound ways that are evident to those around us. His presence leaves no one unmarked.

Margot Starbuck, author of *The Girl in the Orange Dress*, told me her story of finding His face.

Life's circumstances had led me to believe that I was unlovable.

Specifically, being given up for adoption at birth, enduring violence in my childhood home, living with my father's alcoholism and my parents' divorces had convinced me, in my deepest places, that I wasn't *worth* loving.

As a young mother, I was certain that a God who "gave his only son"—under the false pretense of "loving the world," no less—was no better than the father who'd given me up, the one who hurt my mom, or the ones who drank too much. Finally, raising my fist to God, I accused God of being like all the rest.

Desperate, I demanded to know where a single reliable human face, to whom I might have turned in childhood, had been.

"One face," I pleaded. "Where was that one face, when I was young, that was entirely *for* me?"

Suddenly, into my agony, God whispered two words, "I am."

The force and clarity surprised me.

Then two more words, "...*for* you."

I am for you.

As I heard the words, the eyes of my heart turned to see an image of Jesus hanging on the Cross. In that holy moment, God assured me, "I love you *so* much, that I do not seek my own life at your expense. I am altogether *for* you. In fact, I give my *own life* out of my great love for you."

As I came to realize, in my bones, that Jesus had given Himself on my behalf, I at last knew that I was *worth* loving. That moment of understanding, of course, didn't happen in isolation. Instead, my eyes were opened to the ways that the members of Christ's body had been used, *for years*, as God's holy agents in my life. In the same way that Jesus had given flesh to the father's love, members of his body had made his love real to me, reflecting the truth about who I was. I was at last set free.

That hard-won freedom liberated me to do the thing I was made to do: love God and others. No longer bound by lies, convinced of my inherent worth as God's beloved, I'd been set free to be *for* others, especially the weak, the way that God had been *for* me.

In the end—and from the beginning—we learn who we are, and what we're worth, from the faces around us. It's the way we're wired. Thankfully, the Face that does not fail has been seen and heard and known in the person of Jesus, speaking truth to every human heart, insisting, "I am *for* you."

REFLECTIVE FACES

We not only read each others' faces, we reflect them. Next time you're in deep conversation with someone, notice how the two of you begin to unconsciously reflect each other's facial expressions. Or watch two people who have had a long and intimate relationship. They make similar faces to express certain things. My sons now will often say to me, "You just made a Dad face!" as an expression that reflects my late husband's spreads across my face. The more intimate the connection, the more you begin to reflect each other's faces. You've heard it said that long-married couples start to look alike. Not because their physical features change, but because they begin to reflect each other's facial expressions.

When Moses's face reflected the glory of the Lord, it was temporary. Because it was a glory that came from the outside, it faded away. Jesus, on the mount of His Transfiguration, showed us that He reflected the Lord's glory from the inside. Though that glory was not always visible in the same way it was in that event, it did not fade. It had to be veiled, like Moses's face.

When we are face-to-face with the Lord, we absorb His glory and then reflect it like a mirror. This glory comes from the inside. It is not a temporary or cosmetic change. It is a structural change. We are being changed into the same likeness, from one degree of glory to the next.

HIS VOICE

That Hebrew word *payim*—faces or presence—has an interesting etymology. It means faces or countenance, but it also means "to ask or inquire from." Its literal meaning is "to meet at the mouth," i.e., see what someone will say. What does God have to say? "This is my Son, whom I love; with him I am well pleased. Listen to him!" (Matthew 17:5). See what He has to say. Meet at His mouth.

Face-to-face, we can hear Him clearly. My mother has trouble hearing, but if you face her, then she can hear you. Something about the voice coming directly from your face to hers eliminates the distortions that occur when those sound waves travel a roundabout path to her ear. The Lord invites you to meet at His mouth. Hear His direct voice.

SEEKING HIS PRESENCE

"'You will seek me and find me when you seek me with all your heart. I will be found by you,' declares the LORD" (Jeremiah 29:13–14). Notice the sentence structure. Not "you will find me," but rather, "I will be found by you." If we seek Him, He will do the being found. He has made Himself easy to find. He is not hiding. He is pursuing us, wooing us, seeking us. When we seek Him, we find that we are responding to one who has been seeking us.

The word *seek* tells us that there is an active component to our longing for God. We must seek Him. We have to open our lives actively to His presence. We don't have to chase Him down, or seek Him out from some distant location. We do, though, have to seek Him.

Seeking Him means actively positioning our lives so that we are available to Him. I love the responses of Abraham and Moses when they heard the Lord's voice: "Here I am." Many times through the day, I just say, "Here I am." He doesn't need help finding me, but rather I'm expressing my willingness to be used by Him. I'm at His beck and call. When you hear Him calling your name, just say, "Here I am." How do you know He is calling your name? Just the fact that your attention swung to Him is all the proof you need. He is always calling your name.

The spiritual disciplines, such as prayer, Bible reading, meditation, fasting, and celebration, are critical. That is how we keep our lives open to His voice and His supernatural work. Just be in position and He will speak. He has so many ways to speak to you that you can't set up an expectation of what it feels like when God speaks. You can't compare how He speaks to someone else with how He speaks to you. You can't compare how He spoke last time to how He is speaking this time. Just relax and know that He is speaking and you are hearing. Don't struggle and strain. Just rest.

We need to be intimately connected to the body of Christ— His church. That goes beyond church attendance. It is important to find small groups of believers with whom you can communicate on deep levels. Being involved with the body of Christ is essential to hearing Him clearly. Together, you meet at His mouth. You hear one aspect, and someone else hears another, and together the voice of the Lord becomes clear.

During my many years involved in a small prayer group, I have noticed a consistent phenomenon. Often, the listening comes in the speaking. As we start to express our prayers in words, we find ourselves praying things that we had not thought before. And one person's prayer flows into the prayer of another, like suddenly we are on the same wavelength. God expresses His voice through us in ways that are unexpected.

I've experienced it too many times to think it is a unique experience. There is a way that God speaks among us that is powerful and is different from how He speaks to us individually. Listen both ways if you want to hear Him clearly.

WORLD-CHANGING PRESENCE

His presence as your reference point frees you from distorted views of reality.

> *"The LORD bless you*
> *and keep you;*
> *the LORD make his face shine upon you*
> *and be gracious to you;*
> *the LORD turn his face toward you*
> *and give you peace."*
> —Numbers 6:24–26

Transformed by His presence, you will reflect Him in the world. You will become a leader who leads with integrity and courage and passion. You will be free to take the risks that He has called you to in the secret place of His presence.

His presence in our lives takes us into the world, where we act as His ambassadors, inviting others into His presence with us. His presence is the anchor that grounds us and the energy that moves us and the power that enables us.

> *"All authority in heaven and on earth has been given to me. Therefore go and make disciples of all nations, baptizing them in the name of the Father and of the Son and of the Holy Spirit, and teaching them to obey everything I have commanded you. And surely I am with you always, to the very end of the age."*
> —Matthew 28:18–20

> *He has committed to us the message of reconciliation. We are therefore Christ's ambassadors, as though God were making his appeal through us. We implore you on Christ's behalf: Be reconciled to God.*
> —2 Corinthians 5:19–21

Today's missionary movement has its roots in the hearts of men and women who craved the presence of the Lord—a craving that birthed a prayer movement that birthed an outreach that impacted missionary pioneers like William Carey and John Wesley. The tentacles of that single-minded desire to seek the presence of the living Jesus still extend outward from its birthplace, Hernhutt, Germany—the estate of a man named Count Nicolaus Ludwig von Zinzendorf.

Zinzendorf had a motto by which he lived: "I have one passion: it is Jesus, Jesus only." From his childhood, he loved the Lord's presence. In 1722, a group of Protestant refugees, who became known as the Moravians, sought refuge on his estate. As the community grew, so did the problems. Five years after the first refugees arrived, Zinzendorf called the people to a service of communion. At that service, during a time of fervent prayer, a desire for Christ infected the worshipers.

The experience is described this way: "We saw the hand of God and His wonders.... The Holy Ghost came upon us and in those days great signs and wonders took place in our midst.... A great hunger after the Word of God took possession of us so that we had to have three services every day.... Every one desired above everything else that the Holy Spirit might have full control. Self-love and self-will, as well as all disobedience, disappeared and an overwhelming flood of grace swept us all out into the great ocean of Divine Love."

A prayer vigil began that changed the world. On a rotating hourly schedule, at least one person was interceding around the clock, seven days a week, without interruption for 100 years. From that extraordinary focus on the presence of the living Jesus, the modern missionary movement evolved. The Moravians sent out 100 missionaries from their own midst. It was the example of the Moravians that stirred the heart of William Carey and birthed the passion that drove him to the mission fields of India. John and Charles Wesley, sailing to America to become missionaries, found themselves fellow passengers with a group of Moravians. John Wesley credits their example of deep faith as the impetus for his own genuine salvation through grace, the bedrock of what would become an amazingly fruitful life of international ministry.

Truly in Count Zinzendorf's life we see how one person's desire to know the presence of the Lord can unleash the power of the Lord to turn the world upside down. His presence frees us to spend our lives for His sake.

Discussion

1. Identify the ways a face communicates beyond words.

2. How is it different being face-to-face with someone rather than communicating at a distance?

3. Think of people over your lifetime whose presence you now reflect.

4. Review the concepts and identify insights that relate to some or all of the four characteristics of fully free people.

   - Be vehicles through which God's Spirit will be unleashed in the world.

   - Be leaders of influence and uncompromised integrity.

   - Be courageous in their calling and engaged in their culture.

   - Be passionate about God as they step out and take risks together with other believers.

Who for the joy set before him endured the cross, scorning its shame, and sat down at the right hand of the throne of God.

Key 5
His Promise

Promises to Keep

For our sakes, Jesus, who was the darling of heaven — worshiped and honored day and night — chose to take the way of the Cross. He considered our salvation so valuable, that He laid aside His position and His possessions and ran the race marked out for Him.

The outcome of His obedience is that He is now seated at the right hand of the throne of God. Paul puts it in these words:

> *Who, being in very nature God,*
> *did not consider equality with God something to be grasped,*
> *but made himself nothing,*
> *taking the very nature of a servant,*
> *being made in human likeness.*
> *And being found in appearance as a man,*
> *he humbled himself*
> *and became obedient to death—*
> *even death on a cross!*
> *Therefore God exalted him to the highest place*
> *and gave him the name that is above every name,*
> *that at the name of Jesus every knee should bow,*
> *in heaven and on earth and under the earth,*
> *and every tongue confess that Jesus Christ is Lord,*
> *to the glory of God the Father.*
> —Philippians 2:6–11

We are fixing our gaze on Jesus, who stripped down and ran the bruising course that won our salvation. He ran with determination—single-minded in His pursuit, tenacious in His resolve. When He hit the wall, He powered through. He ran to win, and He won the prize. He is seated at the right hand of the Father. Is that the prize? I don't think so. That is what He was willing to leave behind to pursue our salvation. "And now, Father, glorify me in your presence with the glory I had with you before the world began" (John 17:5). He didn't have to win that position. What was the prize? What was Jesus's heart so set on that He "endured the cross, scorning the shame"?

We are the prize. Can you believe it? Read it for yourself. "And God raised us up with Christ and seated us with him in the heavenly realms in Christ Jesus" (Ephesians 2:6–7). The promise that motivated Jesus and kept Him at His task was the promise that we would be seated in the heavenlies with Him. Listen to His impassioned prayer:

> *"I have given them the glory that you gave me, that they may be one as we are one: I in them and you in me. May they be brought to complete unity to let the world know that you sent me and have loved them even as you have loved me. Father, I want those you have given me to be with me where I am, and to see my glory, the glory you have given me because you loved me before the creation of the world."*
> —John 17:22–24

The phrase "I want those you have given me to be with me where I am" could be more literally translated "I want that where I am they may be with me," according to the UBS New Testament Handbook Series. He speaks in a verb tense that means "where I am" at any given moment. Jesus wants us with Him now. Are we seeing His glory right now? Paul says we are: "But we all, with unveiled face, beholding as in a mirror the glory of the Lord" (2 Corinthians 3:18 NASB). Are we with Him right now? We are included in Him and present with Him in the heavenly realms, just as He is in us in the earthly realm.

We have a saying that is meant to demean the value of someone. "She's no prize," we might say sarcastically. Isn't it amazing to know that Jesus thinks just the opposite?

"What a prize you are!" He says to you. "Worth everything you cost Me!"

When Jesus chose to run the race marked out for Him, He did it to obtain a promise. He wasn't running just to run. He was running to win the prize.

THE PURPOSE OF A PROMISE

When God calls us to obedience, He is calling us to embrace a promise. It is the promise that keeps us running the race, powering through the wall. God set it all up so that we would so desire His promise that we would be motivated to run the race set before us.

What is the purpose of a promise? It awakens expectations. It calls attention to possibilities. It motivates. It holds out a goal. A promise can be productive.

God's promises work first by creating a desire in us for what He is offering. Once that desire has been created, then our hearts have been drawn in that direction like a magnet is drawn to the polestar.

I spend many hours on airplanes. Most airplanes are supplied with a catalog in the seat pocket, and this catalog is filled with all kinds of gadgets that are likely to appeal to people who travel often. As I browse the catalog, my attention is often caught by some gadget that promises to make my life easier in some way.

For example, let's say that one day I see in the catalog a set of noise-cancelling earphones. Until that moment, I had no desire for noise-cancelling earphones. Until that moment, I didn't know that noise-cancelling earphones existed. Once I knew they existed, then I began to notice all the noise around me that could be eliminated by noise-cancelling earphones. I had never noticed how loud the world really was! Now, I greatly desired noise-cancelling earphones. Now the promise of quiet—which before would have seemed like a fantasy—seemed possible. I had to have quiet! How could I get quiet? By possessing noise-cancelling earphones. It was not the earphones I craved, but the cancelled noise that the earphones promised.

By presenting me with the possibility of quiet, a desire for quiet was awakened. The promise of quiet could be realized by purchasing the earphones. As soon as I reached out and took hold of the promise—paid for the earphones in this case—the promise could be mine in experience. I had to let go of cash to get possession of the earphones. Though my cash is valuable to me, I believed the earphones to be even more valuable. Worth the letting go.

God makes promises to us for much the same reason. He is letting us know what He has available, if only we will ask. His promises are meant to ignite faith and expectation and desire, and ultimately point us to Him. His promises act to bind our hearts to His. His promises turn our eyes toward Him.

Peter says that God has given us His great and precious promises and that through these promises we can partake of the divine nature and escape the corruption that is in the world. Everything we need for life or godliness is ours in the form of promises God has made. (See 2 Peter 1:3–4.)

A promise might be compared to a check that needs to be cashed. The check itself is not the end. There is a reality that stands behind the check. The check says that the money is available and can be claimed. The check says that the owner of the assets has given the check-bearer access to those assets. This is what Paul affirms when he said, "For no matter how many promises God has made, they are 'Yes' in Christ" (2 Corinthians 1:20). God doesn't make empty promises or write bad checks. Jesus is the reality that stands behind every promise God has ever made. "My God will meet all your needs according to his glorious riches *in Christ Jesus*" (Philippians 4:19, emphasis mine). "Christ, *in whom* are hidden all the treasures of wisdom and knowledge" (Colossians 2:2–3, emphasis mine).

Let's examine 2 Peter 1:3 in more detail. Read it through again.

"His divine power has given us everything we need for life and godliness through our knowledge of him who called us by his own glory and goodness. Through these he has given us his very great and precious promises, so that through them you may participate in the divine nature and escape the corruption in the world caused by evil desires" (2 Peter 1:3–4).

I'm going to dig in to the language here. We'll mine the Greek for clearer understanding of what Peter is communicating. His power—which operates in us through the indwelling Jesus—"*has given us* everything we need for life (*zoe*) and godliness (Christ-likeness)." The word translated "given" means "to grant or bestow." Its verb tense means an action completed in the past and now active in the present. It is in the full possession of the receiver. You already have in your possession everything you need for life and godliness because His power has imparted it to you.

How is this power activated in our lives? "Through our knowledge of him...." By knowing Him. The word translated "knowledge" means to know by experience and personal observation, to understand. When we know Jesus in a present-tense, intimate relationship, everything we need for life and godliness is functioning in our lives.

Jesus's own glory and goodness—the beauty of who Jesus is—has called out to our hearts and attracted and wooed us to Himself. He has given—granted or bestowed—*very great* and *precious* promises. Why give us these promises? *So that* through them we may "participate in the divine nature." Did you get that? We participate in the divine nature.

He imparts Himself to us, making us colaborers with Him. We yield ourselves to Him so that He can impart Himself to us and express Himself through us to the world.

When we are living in the active power of His very great and precious promises, we are living in the power of the divine nature. In order to cling to and embrace the living, indwelling Jesus (the divine nature), we necessarily have to flee from (escape) the corruption of the world. We can't cling to both. It's one or the other.

Peter suggests that there is a natural response to knowing about the great and precious promises:

For this very reason, make every effort to add to your faith goodness; and to goodness, knowledge; and to knowledge, self-control; and to self-control, perseverance; and to perseverance, godliness; and to godliness, brotherly kindness; and to brotherly kindness, love. For if you possess these qualities in increasing measure, they will keep you from being ineffective and unproductive in your knowledge of our Lord Jesus Christ.
—2 Peter 1:5–9

Paul similarly lays out the promise of the indwelling Christ in 2 Corinthians 6:16–18: "I will live with them and walk among them, and I will be their God and they will be my people" And then he puts forth our response, "Therefore come out . . . and be separate. . . . Touch no unclean thing." He later continues: "Since we have these promises, dear friends, let us purify ourselves from everything that contaminates body and spirit, perfecting holiness out of reverence for God" (2 Corinthians 7:1). We see again the dichotomy in the command, "make every effort to enter this rest."

In both of these parallel teachings, one from Peter and the other from Paul, the promise is the indwelling life of Christ, which guarantees all the promises. Our response is to commit ourselves fully to choosing Spirit over flesh over and over until it becomes our automatic response. When we compare what God has promised to what the world promises, like Moses before us, we will choose the glory of Christ over the glitter of the world.

THE PROMISER

A promise is only as good as the person who makes it. The character of the promiser is what gives the promise its value.

As we learn to embrace God's promises, the starting point is the nature of God. The essence of God's character is in itself a promise. Who He is determines what He will do and how He will act. Through the Scripture, each time God reveals something of His nature, He is promising us that He will be true to that nature in any circumstance. Sometimes the promises of God don't come packaged in declarative statements, but instead are implied in the revelation of His being.

God has always dealt with His people by communicating promises to them. By promising first, then performing what He has promised, He awakens in us the desire and expectation that find their outlet in obedience. His promises prompt obedience.

God's commands and His call come with promises. He never calls us to an action just for the action's sake, but for what the active obedience will lead to. It will always lead to greater freedom.

> *I run in the path of your commands,*
> *for you have set my heart free.*
> —Psalm 119:32

> *I will walk about in freedom,*
> *for I have sought out your precepts.*
> —Psalm 119:45

Obedience will always result in a deeper experience of the indwelling Jesus. Read His promise to you.

> *"As the Father has loved me, so have I loved you. Now remain in my love. If you obey my commands, you will remain in my love, just as I have obeyed my Father's commands and remain in his love. I have told you this so that my joy may be in you and that your joy may be complete."*
> —John 15:9–12

> *"Whoever has my commands and obeys them, he is the one who loves me. He who loves me will be loved by my Father, and I too will love him and show myself to him."*
> —John 14:21

Run your race with your eyes on the prize. You are the prize that kept Jesus to His task. He is the Prize that holds your heart steadfast. He is the Promise that gives you the motivation to power through. Have you hit the wall? Do you need incentive to keep going when you want to give up? More of Him in your experience! More of Him flowing through you into your world! That's the prize. He is the Promise

Discussion

1. What motivated Jesus to run His race and power through the wall?

2. What is the purpose of a promise?

3. What is the essence of all the promises of God, wrapped into one grand promise?

4. Review the concepts and identify insights that relate to some or all of the four characteristics of fully free people.

   - Be vehicles through which God's Spirit will be unleashed in the world.

   - Be leaders of influence and uncompromised integrity.

   - Be courageous in their calling and engaged in their culture.

   - Be passionate about God as they step out and take risks together with other believers.

Life Unhindered!

CHAPTER 13

Promise Me

The entire Scripture is a promise, explicitly stated or implied. Where it reveals the power of God, it implies that power will work in our lives. Where it reveals the character of God, it implies the promise of who He will be in our lives. Where it demonstrates His love, it implies the promise that we will experience that love. Whatever His Word reveals about who He is or what He does, He is promising.

Every command He gives has a corresponding promise. He created us and knows us and understands that "because I said so" only goes so far. Indeed, we will obey Him just because He said so. We will obey Him without the clear understanding of where this obedience will lead exactly. But the reason we will obey Him just because He said so, is because we know His "say so" always has a purpose behind it.

As we close this study on living life unhindered, we focus on the final key: His promise. What frees us to let go of the sins and hindrances and attachments that weigh us down? We are freed from our natural reluctance to let go—freed from the tendency to work against our own best interests—by the prize set before us, Jesus Himself. We are His prize, and He is ours. We are freed from being mastered by the mundane by the power of the promise.

As the Israelites were fleeing Egypt, God told Moses to raise his staff and stretch out his hand over the sea to divide the water. Why? *So that the Israelites could go through the sea on dry ground.*

After His people crossed over safely, then the Lord told Moses again to stretch out his hand over the sea. Why? *So that the waters may flow back over the Egyptians and their chariots and horsemen.* The end result of all this was that the people feared the Lord and put their trust in Him and in Moses, His servant. (See Exodus 14:31.)

Telling Moses to hold out his rod might have seemed to be an arbitrary command, except for the accompanying promise. Command and promise becomes obedience and provision. Every hindrance is swept away, engulfed and overpowered by the flood of God's power. Where there was no way, a way appears. A life of obedience is a life unhindered.

PROMISES, PROMISES

Let's just take some time to marinate in His promises. Watch for the command-promise principle. See it turn into obedience-provision.

In the following examples, the promise and the command are fairly obvious. Look for the pattern. Take hold of the promise by submitting to the command. Let these words make their home in you. God is a Promiser. Always has been and always will be. Highlight the command in one color, and the accompanying promise in another.

> *"But seek first his kingdom and his righteousness, and all these things will be given to you as well."*
> —Matthew 6:33–34

> *"I tell you that if two of you on earth agree about anything you ask for, it will be done for you by my Father in heaven. For where two or three come together in my name, there am I with them."*
> —Matthew 18:19–20

Life Unhindered!

"Give, and it will be given to you. A good measure, pressed down, shaken together and running over, will be poured into your lap. For with the measure you use, it will be measured to you."
—Luke 6:38

"If you remain in me and my words remain in you, ask whatever you wish, and it will be given you. This is to my Father's glory, that you bear much fruit, showing yourselves to be my disciples."
—John 15:7–8

"But when you fast, put oil on your head and wash your face, so that it will not be obvious to men that you are fasting, but only to your Father, who is unseen; and your Father, who sees what is done in secret, will reward you."
—Matthew 6:17–18

*"Bring the whole tithe into the storehouse, that there may be food in my house. Test me in this," says the L*ORD *Almighty, "and see if I will not throw open the floodgates of heaven and pour out so much blessing that you will not have room enough for it. I will prevent pests from devouring your crops, and the vines in your fields will not cast their fruit," says the L*ORD *Almighty. "Then all the nations will call you blessed, for yours will be a delightful land," says the L*ORD *Almighty."*
—Malachi 3:10–12

Rejoice in the Lord always. I will say it again: Rejoice! Let your gentleness be evident to all. The Lord is near. Do not be anxious about anything, but in everything, by prayer and petition, with thanksgiving, present your requests to God. And the peace of God, which transcends all understanding, will guard your hearts and your minds in Christ Jesus.
—Philippians 4:4–7

Finally, brothers, whatever is true, whatever is noble, whatever is right, whatever is pure, whatever is lovely, whatever is admirable— if anything is excellent or praiseworthy—think about such things. Whatever you have learned or received or heard from me, or seen

in me—put it into practice. And the God of peace will be with you.
—Philippians 4:8–9

In your anger do not sin; when you are on your beds, search your hearts and be silent. Offer right sacrifices and trust in the LORD.... You have filled my heart with greater joy than when their grain and new wine abound. I will lie down and sleep in peace, for you alone, O LORD, make me dwell in safety.
—Psalm 4:4–8

"If anyone would come after me, he must deny himself and take up his cross daily and follow me. For whoever wants to save his life will lose it, but whoever loses his life for me will save it."
—Luke 9:23–25

"Then the King will say to those on his right, 'Come, you who are blessed by my Father; take your inheritance, the kingdom prepared for you since the creation of the world. For I was hungry and you gave me something to eat, I was thirsty and you gave me something to drink, I was a stranger and you invited me in, I needed clothes and you clothed me, I was sick and you looked after me, I was in prison and you came to visit me.'"
—Matthew 25:34–36

The LORD helps them and delivers them; he delivers them from the wicked and saves them, because they take refuge in him.
—Psalm 37:40

Brothers, I do not consider myself yet to have taken hold of it. But one thing I do: Forgetting what is behind and straining toward what is ahead, I press on toward the goal to win the prize for which God has called me heavenward in Christ Jesus.
—Philippians 3:13–14

FINDING THE DESIRE OF YOUR HEART

Your heart was made for Him. Your heart longs for Him. All the things we think we want are just cheap substitutes for His presence.

My hungry heart cries out for You.
No earthly substitute will do.
My life consumed, Your Life the Flame
That leaves me nevermore the same.
A heart like Yours, my one desire.
Do Your work, Refiner's Fire.

All of our longing is for Him. The more we live face-to-face with Him, the more we find every promise wrapped up in one: His presence. "Now the Lord is the Spirit, and where the Spirit of the Lord is, *there is freedom*" (2 Corinthians 3:17, emphasis mine).

Everything He has created us to crave is revealed in the promise of His presence. Every desire our hearts hold is satisfied in His presence. In His presence we find joy and gladness (see Psalm 21:6).

Let the presence of the Lord be your daily destination. It doesn't matter where you are or what you're doing, you can be in the presence of God. He is seeking you out. He is drawing you to Himself. You only need to respond. He is right there inside you, wooing you and inviting you to turn away from yourself and toward Him.

God's presence doesn't change. He is always fully present to you. You, however, are not always fully present to Him. Make it your determined goal to live with an awareness of Him.

One more story. Rees Howells's call took him from his home in Wales to the mission fields of South Africa in the early twentieth century, where he was instrumental in a great spiritual awakening. He then founded a Bible college in Wales to train others for the mission field. This far-reaching ministry was the outgrowth of an experience Howells had in which he heard Jesus's request to possess him fully. Howells tells the story of that transforming moment in his words:

> "He won my love—every bit of it. He broke me and everything in me went right out to Him.... Then He spoke to me and said, 'Behold, I stand at the door and knock. May I come in to you...? Will you accept

me?' 'Yes,' I replied, and He came in and that moment everything was changed. I was born into another world. I found myself in the Kingdom of God, and the Creator became my Father....

When you receive the Savior, you receive the love of God. That love flooded my being, and it has flooded my being ever since.... I saw that by His coming in to me, He would love sinners through me, as He loved me. It would not be forcing myself to love others any more than the Savior forced Himself to love me."
—Rees Howells, as quoted in Norman Grubb's *Rees Howells, Intercessor*

Rees Howells, living in the awareness of the indwelling, eternal presence of God, walked out into the world and the Father loved the world through him every day of his life.

Finally, look at Jesus. How did He live His life among us? He lived in response to the Father, continually aware of His presence.

"I tell you the truth, the Son can do nothing by himself; he can do only what he sees his Father doing, because whatever the Father does the Son also does. For the Father loves the Son and shows him all he does" (John 5:19–20).

When we look at Jesus, we see a life lived in the presence of the Father. The Father's presence was a constant for Jesus. The words He spoke, the miracles He performed, the choices He made—all were the outflow of the Father's presence.

Today God dwells in us. His presence is His gift to us, the prize worth every effort.

THE KEYS TO WALKING IN FREEDOM

God has designed the process of your full-spectrum salvation so that it requires that you be attentive to Him always. He's taking you to a place He'll show you. Your freedom is His goal. Everything you need to walk in freedom, He has already provided. Your challenge is to learn how to access the keys He has set before you and open the door to walking in freedom.

Freedom to be *altared*. Freedom from all the things that hold us back. Freedom to live out all He's called us to. All because He promises us Himself. And with that Treasure ever before us, we can be vehicles through which the Spirit flows to others, we can be leaders of influence, we can courageously be engaged in our culture, and we can be passionate risk-takers for His kingdom.

Discussion

1. Review the five keys to walking in freedom and state your understanding of each.

2. Review the four characteristics of fully free people.

3. Identify people in your life who have been God's platform, showing you His faithfulness. Who are your own faith heroes who have shaped your concept of God?

Experiencing the Scriptures

by Caroline Lawson Dean

Experiential approach: These immersion exercises enable participants to encounter the Scriptures through a new medium. Each new experience is geared to enhance your discussion of *Life Unhindered!* and Hebrews 11–12.

If you choose to use this guide in a retreat format:

Obviously, retreat participants should read the book in advance. The first section, "Imitating the Heroes of the Faith," should be done together as a large group. There are at least two options for the other sections. They could be done in order all together with breakout groups where called for. Or they could be set up as stations in different rooms, with participants choosing different activities to participate in during specified times throughout the retreat. At the end of each station, groups can also discuss the questions at the end of each chapter. Hopefully the experiential exercises create more fruitful discussion. (Note: Some stations are more time-consuming than others and so leaders should plan accordingly. These activities in total would make for a very full daylong retreat; two days are preferred. If the social justice activity for chapter 12 is to be done during the retreat, not just researched, then two days are necessary.)

If you choose to use this guide in a Bible study format:

Bible study leaders should assign two or three chapters of *Life Unhindered* at a time, which allows two or three options of stations for the participants each week. Six weeks is probably optimal for the entire study. Remember some activities take longer than others. Some participants may only complete one activity; others may be able to do a couple. Allow an hour and a half to two hours together. Again, at the end of each station, leaders can facilitate dialogue based on the discussion guides at the end of each chapter. (Note: It would benefit participants to know ahead of time about the details of certain stations.)

CHAPTERS 1, 2, AND 3—IMITATING THE HEROES OF THE FAITH—A THEATRICAL OPTION

Supplies needed: Bibles, Scripture references for the scenes referenced from the Old Testament, and enough space for the groups to brainstorm and perform a short skit.

Leaders should tell the gathered large group: "These questions are meant to spark discussion and interactive learning. There are no right answers. Fruitful discussion is the goal."

Then the leader should divide the large group into groups of three or four people. Assign each group a hero or heroine of the faith. Leaders should then explain that each group has 20 minutes to:

1. Develop a 3-minute skit that "modernizes" the hero and his or her situation in Scripture. Prepare to act out the short vignette illustrating the characteristics of this hero's faith in a modern context.

2. Discuss the following questions about your hero from Hebrews 11:

   • What could have hindered the hero's faith? Think about the scenario you imagined and what unforeseen issues could arise if the scene were to play out for longer than 3 minutes.

   • What does the relationship between this hero and God tell us about the character of God?

- If you could ask your hero one question, what would it be?

3. Share your skit with the group and discuss your brief answers to the questions above.

CHAPTERS 4—A CRITICAL REFLECTION— A BRAINSTORMING OPTION

Supplies needed: a whiteboard or poster boards and markers for brainstorming in a group.

1. How does your Christian community, small group, or church sometimes create:

   - Shame?

   - Legalism?

   - Staking of your identity in the world?

   - Staking of your identity in the ones whom you love?

   - Staking of your identity in the past?

2. How does your Christian community, small group, or church free people from these habits of thought?

Brainstorm ways to cultivate these liberating practices in your community.

CHAPTER 5—RESOLVED—A PRACTICAL OPTION

Supplies needed: Bibles, notebooks or journals.

Jennifer Kennedy Dean writes, "The famous eighteenth-century American pastor Jonathan Edwards compiled a list of resolutions that spelled out how he would live with eternity in focus rather than be tossed about by life's changing circumstances. Let me commend a few to you" (p. 98).

Write out a list of resolutions that will help you lay aside hindrances that weigh you down and distract you from the race. Use Jonathan Edwards's list and the follow-up points given by Jennifer Kennedy Dean. Discuss together as a group which resolutions will be most difficult and why.

CHAPTER 6—LECTIO DIVINA— A MEDITATIVE OPTION

Supplies needed: Bibles and paper for journaling.

Jennifer Kennedy Dean writes, "The first way that Jesus begins to clean us out inside is by speaking His Word in His present-tense, living voice. When you read the Scripture, when you meditate on the Scripture, and memorize the Scripture, hear His voice speaking to you" (page 111).

Choose a group leader to facilitate the time of reflection. The group leader should go over the format of reflection before they start. In a small group, meditate prayerfully on Hebrews 12:1–2 in this format:

- The group leader asks one person to read Hebrews 12:1–2 out loud, slowly and carefully.

- The group sits in silence for a moment of reflection.

- Then the group leader instructs them to listen for a word or phrase that sticks out to them as the passage is read again.

- Another person reads the passage out loud.

- After a moment of reflection, each person in the group shares the word, phrase, or sentence that resonates with him or her. All participants should have the opportunity to do this, but no one should feel pressured.

- Instruct the group to listen again for how the word, phrase, or passage speaks to their lives directly. Or how they hear the passage in a new way. The group leader reads the passage out loud for the last time.

- After a longer time of silence, the group leader should then invite participants to share how they hear this passage in a new way or how it speaks to their lives.

- Finally, end with silence and prayer.

(Note: Group members can be encouraged to journal during the times of silent reflection and meditation.)

CHAPTER 7—MEDLEY—A MUSICAL OPTION

Supplies needed: access to musical instruments or inform participants to bring their own instruments.

Musically illustrate the idea of *perseverance* in Hebrews 12:1–2, either by composing an original piece—allowing all of the members of the group to participate—or by creating a medley with pieces that are already composed.

Or you can also look to theater and create a dance or musical interpretation related to the theme of perseverance. This can be based upon existing musicals. Present this creative interpretation in front of the large group.

If composing or performing a musical piece is too difficult or intimidating, the group can work together to collect and analyze different songs (instrumental or with lyrics) that relate to the theme of perseverance.

Chapter 8—Pottery—A Tactile Option

Supplies needed: moldable clay.

On pages 135–136, Jennifer Kennedy Dean writes:

> How often our pride...causes us to think of our wounds
> and our scars as something to hide; something ugly;
> something demeaning; something that lessens our value.
> But look at Jesus. Look at what Jesus thought of His
> wounds: "Here, Thomas. Look at My wounds. Touch
> My scars. These are proof of My resurrection. I bear
> the marks of death, but I am alive!" Jesus knew His
> wounds were beautiful....
>
> At the places where I am broken, the power of Christ
> is authenticated in me for others. Where I have submit-
> ted to the crucifixion, the power of the resurrection is on
> display. I can say, "Look at my wounds. Touch my scars.
> I have death-wounds, but I am alive." I can wear my
> wounds without shame. They tell a resurrection story.

Illustrate Jennifer Kennedy Dean's image of a beautiful broken
jar or beautiful scars by molding a piece of clay. Share together
how your piece of pottery conveys your interpretation of the
depth and dark beauty of brokenness.

Chapter 9—Videography— A Cinematic Option

Supplies needed: either digital cameras or a video camera; resources
to edit and display the images.

Take a video camera (or regular digital camera) and search for
two or three scenes in nature, in a home, in a church, etc., that
capture the essence of Hebrews 12:1–2 for you. Try to illustrate
these verses with short video clips or photographs (e.g., clouds,
a runner, things that entangle, etc.). If you have the correct edit-
ing software and resources, share the visual images with the

entire group. (Note: This activity could also be done with a Polaroid camera for a fun retro twist.)

CHAPTER 10—VISUALIZING GOD'S DWELLING PLACE—A SPATIAL OPTION

Supplies needed: poster-size construction paper, colored pencils.

Jennifer Kennedy Dean writes, "When God comes to take up residence in you, He makes His home in your spirit. That is His Holy of Holies. Immediately, His presence makes your spirit holy. But your soul—the sanctuary—is still full of leftover flesh and sin. He begins a restoration project, restoring your soul to its intended purpose. It is to be the place where His glory is displayed" (p. 163).

Take a few minutes to discuss as a group: How does God display Himself in your soul? What renovation projects are going on in your temple? Draw a visual representation of yourself as God's "dwelling place." Try to illustrate the ways that God uses your temple to display His glory and draw a visual representation of the ways that God is renovating your soul. Share with the group.

CHAPTER 11—DIALOGUING ABOUT SCRIPTURE— A COMMUNAL OPTION

Supplies needed: Bibles.

Jennifer Kennedy Dean writes, "Being involved with the body of Christ is essential to hearing Him clearly. Together, you meet at His mouth. You hear one aspect, and someone else hears another, and together the voice of the Lord becomes clear" (p. 172).

Practice reading Hebrews 12:1–2 as a community. Discuss what the text means to you personally.

- What does it remind you of in your life? Are you a runner?

- Does it remind you of other Scriptures?

- If you could ask one question about the text, what would you ask?

Share the answers to these questions in a group and reflect on how you have enlightened each other's understanding of the text.

CHAPTER 12—SERVICE— A SOCIAL JUSTICE OPTION

Supplies needed: Internet access.

Introduce the session by reading Philippians 2:6–11 together and discuss how to emulate the life of Christ as He empties Himself to become a slave to others. Get together in your group and brainstorm a list of God's promises. Think back on some of the missionary stories in *Life Unhindered!* Discuss how these missionaries emptied themselves in order to convey God's promises to poor, oppressed, and lost people groups.

Then come up with a project to do together where you can embody those promises for a group of people who are on the margins of our society (for example: the homeless, the terminally ill, the immigrants, the imprisoned, the mentally ill, or the poor). On the Internet, research the problems these people face in your community.

Lastly, on the Internet, research local service opportunities that are related to your service project. Contact them and work alongside them. Or your church already may be involved in these areas of service, so you could join in existing ministries.

CHAPTER 13—COLLAGE—A VISUAL OPTION

Supplies needed: a stack of diverse magazines, glue sticks, scissors, and large construction paper.

Create a collage of symbols that illustrate the Scriptures (promises) at the end of chapter 13. Find a symbol for each passage and discuss in your group why each image is associated with each passage.

FINAL ACTIVITY—MENTAL IMAGES— AN ARTISTIC OPTION

Supplies needed: paint, colored pencils, magazines, construction paper, and other artistic mediums.

Bring the group back together or talk in small groups about the principles Jennifer Kennedy Dean outlines in *Life Unhindered!* Specifically, discuss how the five keys she references help us shed hindrances in our lives. Then discuss how being *altared* by Christ leads us to live out the four characteristics of truly free people. Allow participants to brainstorm applications individually and as a group.

Take a moment to visualize one of these freeing principles (five keys or four characteristics) and have everyone draw a picture of the "mental image" that comes to them. Share the pictures together in the group.

New Hope® Publishers is a division of WMU®, an
international organization that challenges Christian believers
to understand and be radically involved in God's mission. For
more information about WMU, go to www.wmu.com. More
information about New Hope books may be found at
www.newhopepublishers.com. New Hope books may be
purchased at your local bookstore.

unhindered!

WMU 2010-2011 Emphasis Book

If you've been blessed by this book, we would like to hear your story.
The publisher and author welcome your comments and
suggestions at: newhopereader@wmu.org.

More Outstanding Books
for Unhindered Living

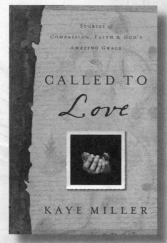
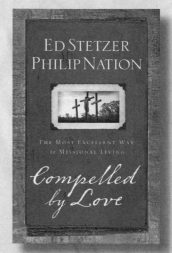
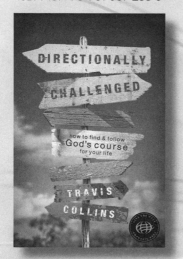